The Sanctity of Life

Volume II

Individuality and the New Society

EDITED BY Abraham Kaplan

University of Washington Press
SEATTLE AND LONDON

Reed College
PORTLAND, OREGON

Portions of "Dissenting Youth and the New Society" by Kenneth Keniston have been published in *The American Scholar,* 37, No. 2 (Spring 1968), 227–45.

Portions of "Biological Determinants of Individuality" by René Dubos have been published in *Environmental Influences,* ed. David C. Glass (New York: The Rockefeller University Press and Russell Sage Foundation, 1968), pp. 138–54.

Copyright © 1970 by the University of Washington Press
"Prejudice and Politics in the American Past and Present" by Seymour Martin Lipset copyright © 1969 by Seymour Martin Lipset
Library of Congress Catalog Card Number 72–103294
Printed in the United States of America

Contents

Introduction   DANIEL H. LABBY   vii

Perspectives on the Theme
   ABRAHAM KAPLAN   3

Dissenting Youth and the New Society
   KENNETH KENISTON   21

Present Discontents of the Student Age Group
   LIONEL ROBBINS   50

The Market versus the Bureaucrat
   MILTON FRIEDMAN   69

Prejudice and Politics in the American Past and Present
   SEYMOUR MARTIN LIPSET   89

Biological Determinants of Individuality
   RENÉ DUBOS   148

Concluding Remarks   ABRAHAM KAPLAN   160

Introduction

DANIEL H. LABBY

Meeting three years ago to draft this second symposium, the planning committee realized that the troubled national scene of 1967 was little different from that of 1965 (described in the introduction to *Life or Death,* the first volume of the series) when they had planned the first conference and selected "Sanctity of Life" as a theme. The same problems were very much in evidence, and if anything, more intense and dispiriting. The unpopular and threatening war had by then escalated "insanely" and produced national disunity, bringing worldwide criticism of America and the policies of the Johnson administration. The dissent of youth and campus revolt were at a peak, and the problems of racism, violence, rioting, and poverty amidst affluence displayed us to the world as a country of less than wholly united states. At times we seemed to be living a part of a Grand Guignol as our leaders stood in front of this horrifying backdrop to tell us that there were already too many people in the country, although more were being born at an ungovernable rate, and that we were fouling our nest by environmental pollution. In addition our economic base was being threatened by recession from the cavortings of a capricious market and a military-industrial complex of dubious respectability.

In contemporary society, scientific and technological advances in the natural, medical, and social sciences were allegedly freeing man from traditional physical, social, and psychological bonds. Had these advances instead created new forms of bondage and produced grave threats to the integrity of the individual? If so, where *was* the individual man in all of this? What was happening to his opportunity? Professor Edward Shils had already noted in the first symposium[1] that "The sanctity of individuality is a variant form of the sanctity of life." Yet individual autonomy seemed threatened on a variety of fronts: the increasing mastery of basic processes governing human growth and behavior, the development and steady use of drugs affecting the mind, the growth of the arts of creating and manipulating large and complex economic and political systems, the threatening obsolescence of social institutions that have traditionally structured the free determination of one's life. Shils had asked a fundamental question:

How is the human race as we have known it, with all its deficiencies, to be protected from the murderous and manipulative wickedness of some of its members and from the passionate curiosity and the

[1] *Life or Death: Ethics and Options* (Seattle: Reed College and University of Washington Press, 1968), pp. 6, 32.

Introduction

scientific and technological genius of others? Each of these major factors working alone would have raised questions about the grounds on which one man's life or individuality may be interfered with, changed, or discontinued, and the factors which might extend or restrict such acts of intervention. Their confluence renders it desirable to consider the whole problem more closely. This is why we ask the questions as to whether life is sacred and as to how far morality permits and how far the law should allow us to intervene into reproduction, the course of life, and the constitution of individuality and privacy.

Challenged to define society's ethical posture in these matters, the planning committee decided that a search-and-identify mission for the individual and his opportunity in our new society would be worth undertaking, and a second symposium was proposed. This was again made possible by the encouragement and generous support of Bess Kaiser Hospital, whose sponsorship had proven so successful for the first conference in 1966.

Once more the Reed College campus was the setting. With its climate of free inquiry and emphasis on individual responsibility, a more congenial intellectual mooring could hardly be desired. The college itself was in transition between presidencies, and a general atmosphere of movement and excitement dominated the community. Victor Rosenblum, then president-elect, came from Northwestern University to attend. He must have sensed something of the uniqueness of Reed through the eyes of the conference, because in his inaugural speech, one year later, he stated: "Since Reed's founding, our emphasis has been on individuality and excellence. Though we have grown in size . . . , we have never seen it as our function to engage in the molding of mass men; the thought that processing of persons could be viewed as an educational function has been an anathema to us. Our concept of teaching, our curriculum, our requirements of our students in conferences, seminars and personal encounters, and our demands of ourselves as instructors and scholars bespeak a rigorous and critical focus on the development and responsibility of the individual." Further in his speech he stated, "there are strong wills within individual members of the Reed community and broad differences amongst them. . . . We have many amenities of style but few new amenities of opinion. . . . We feel affection for the richness and diversity of human learning but eschew turning it into an affectation that would convert learning to mass processing. We seek not to mirror the madness that abounds in the world in our time but to find ways for the resurgence of the sanity of civilization and the sanctity of life."[2]

The selection of the conference participants involved extensive consultation and long debate. The individuals finally chosen were invited less on the basis of their academic disciplines than because they were seminal thinkers who had already offered thoughtful formulations and appraisals of the basic issues concerned with the future of the individual. All

[2] Victor G. Rosenblum, Inaugural Address, Reed College, 16 April 1969.

Introduction

were assigned essentially the same topic and asked to follow their natural drift. Each had already dealt with the problem of individuality in the form of student dissent on his own campus. Indeed, Kenneth Keniston had established a reputation for his studies on personality development in adolescence and early adulthood, and was the author of an authoritative volume, *The Uncommitted: Alienated Youth in American Society,* and more recently of *The Young Radicals.* Lord Lionel C. Robbins, a political economist, was a lifelong teacher and author of the Robbins Report, a plan for strengthening higher education in Great Britain. Seymour Lipset of Harvard University had been viewing contemporary problems in historical perspective as a political sociologist, while Milton Friedman was well known for his approach to the problems of our economy through the preservation of personal freedom and a free market. René Dubos of the Rockefeller University was looking at man as a biological individual, and, as an ecologist, was endeavoring to appraise the total environment and the sociomedical problems of contemporary life.

The word "symposium" means "to drink together," but in the early hours of *this* symposium, except for a common interest in the problems of protesting youth, the participants did not seem to be drinking wine from the same bottle! As a result the papers can be read individually for their unique flavor, and they may be better savored by careful reading than was possible in the hearing. The diverse treatments given the

DANIEL H. LABBY

theme (commented on by Kaplan in his concluding remarks) highlight the individuality of the participants and reinforce the charm of the encounter.

Kaplan's opening perspective gave a general view of the territory to be inspected by the conference. He looked upon the development of individuality as an achievement resulting from integration of the complex different selves contained in every person, suggesting four dimensions of individuality: the psychological, social, political, and the moral or philosophical. Despite this attempt to offer the conference a sober, disciplined instrument, the discussants chose, in their pervasively individual styles, to talk about only one example in Kaplan's system: that of student protest.

It is not surprising that Kaplan distinguishes between identification and identity. Two years before, an Arden House Conference had identified this dilemma as one of the fruits of science: ". . . what does concern many sensitive people, . . . is the fact that the social institution of science is premised on beliefs that may become harmful to man. Jacques Barzun, for one, has expressed the view that the assumption of purposelessness by science is secreting into society something akin to a poison bottled in various brands of existentialism, in the philosophy of the absurd, and in the notion that man reacts automatically to his environment and does not respond creatively to it. The chief method of science is analysis. This means the breaking down 'or cutting up experience for minute study leading to the formulation of relationship' which results in the disappearance of the individual who subse-

Introduction

quently reveals himself only—and pathetically—'as a statistical unit shorn of his unique features.' "[3] This calls to mind a recent piece of charming doggerel:

> My Good Name Is a Number
> These times are somewhat different
> than the Bard's.
> Who steals my purse steals all
> my credit cards,
> including one marked: "Soc.
> Security."
> What then is left of my identity?[4]

At least two dilemmas seem to move through all of Kaplan's consideration. The first is that of recognizing the "need to be needed" as one of the most desperate human needs. Yet as he points out, if we move too close to others we risk the danger of losing individuality, and if we stand too far off then individuality has no meaning: it is loneliness and without love. Kaplan is obliged to conclude "that the more we are involved with others the more of an individual we become": the true meaning and significance of our individual existence seems to be determined by how we reach out and become part of the lives of others. In the Arden House Conference, Clarence C. Walton found poetic instruction for this from Miguel de Unamuno.

[3] Clarence C. Walton (ed.), *Today's Changing Society: A Challenge to Individual Identity* (New York: Institute of Life Insurance, 1967).
[4] Virginia Brasier, "My Good Name Is a Number," *Saturday Review* (10 May 1969), p. 4.

DANIEL H. LABBY

> Give yourself to others: but in order
> to give yourself to them, first dominate
> your neighbor . . . ; in order to dominate
> your neighbor you must know him and love
> him. . . . My endeavor is to impose myself on
> another: to be and to live in him, to make
> him mine—which is the same as making
> myself his—is that which gives meaning to
> religious collectivity, to human solidarity.[5]

A second dilemma occurring in Kaplan's categories is that in the real world action cannot be undertaken singly; that we are indeed, as individuals, obliged to act through collective means. These are dilemmas of our social organization, of our large institutions, including the modern university, and there are moral overtones, as Kaplan points out. Man is accountable morally only for his own acts, but when he acts collectively, the guilt for unreasonable action on the part of one man will fall upon his brother. John W. Gardner noted the magnitude and dimension of such action during the 1969 Godkin Lectures at Harvard.[6] He commented on the need for change in American institutions to make them more responsive, capable of reform and self-renewal—"a hospitable environment for the individual"—and called for collective action to restore individuality by asking men to participate directly in the "reshaping of the institutions that no longer enjoy their

---

[5] Miguel de Unamuno, "The Tragic Sense of Life," quoted in Walton (ed.), *Today's Changing Society.*

[6] "The Individual and Society," Three Godkin Lectures, March 1969. Reported in the *New York Times*, 30 March 1969, and in the *Chronicle of Higher Education*, 3, No. 15 (7 April 1969).

Introduction

confidence." He agreed with the young that individuality is being smothered by the large university and the municipal bureaucracies of cities just as readily as by corporations, but pointed to the benefits of enlarged choices that could and must be offered by large institutions to permit individual fulfillment.

The kind of person who protests is clearly sketched by Kenneth Keniston from direct observations of protesters. Despite their fervidly individual styles of dissent, they are caught in Kaplan's dilemma by being obliged to act as part of a group. But in face of their frustrations they have found it easier to maintain a fixed style and to be certain of their goals. In a more recent expression Keniston has indicated that "what protesting students throughout the world share is the mood more than an ideology or a program, the mood that says that the existing system— the power structure—is hypocritical, unworthy of respect, outmoded, and in urgent need of reform."[7] Keniston has further pointed out that the young suffer a certain sense of stifling of individuality because they have

> come to feel that they live in institutions whose demands lack moral authority or, in the current jargon, "creditability." Today, the moral imperative and urgency behind production, acquisition, materialism and abundance has been lost. Furthermore, with the lack of moral legitimacy felt in the "system" the least request for loyalty, restraint or conformity by its representatives—for example by college presidents and deans—can easily be seen as a moral outrage, and authori-

[7] Kenneth Keniston, "You Have to Grow Up in Scarsdale to Know How Bad Things Really Are," *New York Times*, 27 April 1969.

tarian repression, a manipulative effort to "co-opt" students into joining the Establishment and an exercise in "illegitimate authority" that must be resisted. From this conception springs at least part of the students' vague sense of oppression. And, indeed, perhaps their peculiar feeling of suffocation arises ultimately from living in societies without vital ethical claims.

These feelings of oppression and suffocation can be identified behind the remarks of Lord Robbins. His presentation had been prepared during a period when his own London School of Economics was the object of student unrest for the first time in its long history, which undoubtedly had some influence on the direction of his comments. In a letter to Reed College shortly after the symposium, he offered a progress note on these matters: "I am afraid I have no good news to report about the London School of Economics. We had riots early in the term which led to the place being closed for nearly a month. We are now once again open but sit-ins—and worse, demonstrations—take place nearly every day; and whatever disciplinary measures we can take are hopelessly entangled in a network of obsolete regulation and very hampered legal procedures. I rely on the maxim that 'the trees don't grow up to the sky,' but I can't say that they have stopped growing yet."

Lord Robbins' conservatism was evident in his contributions at the time of the conference. In returning his manuscript in final form fifteen months later, he offered the following addendum:

Introduction

... if news reaches you from this little island you will have learnt that I have been myself over-much concerned with very active manifestations of present discontents of the student age group at the London School of Economics and I have had very little leisure indeed to reflect on past literary enterprises.

I have made no attempt to alter in any way the main argument of the text, nor should I wish to do so. But if I were writing on the same subject now I should of course devote more space to the manifestations of militant violence. ... This paper was written some months before there was any prospect of my becoming Chairman of the Court of Governors at the London School of Economics, at which there have been recent outbursts of student militancy, and no attempt has been made to revise it to take account of the recent manifestations thereof in the United Kingdom.

The contemporary student asks for a piece of the action in the hope of making his bid for a role in providing continuous renewal of our aging institutions, as noted by John W. Gardner. Feeling frustrated and suffocated but highly committed in his own individual style, responding to what he defines as responsibility to the present and future, he is reacting out of a sense of commitment. "Men and women," says Gardner, "taught to cherish a set of values and then trapped in a system that negates those values may react in anger and even violence." The student forced to work within a system so unsympathetic and rigid finds himself under coercion and cannot be expected to learn and prosper. Marianne Moore touched on this point with poetic force over thirty years ago, in "The Student":

DANIEL H. LABBY

>You can't beat hens to
>make them lay. Wolf's wool is the best of wool,
>but it cannot be sheared because
>the wolf will not comply. With knowledge as
>   with wolf's surliness,
>the student studies
>   voluntarily, refusing to be less
>than individual. He
>"gives his opinion and then rests on it;"
>he renders service when there is
>no reward, and is too reclusive for
>   some things to seem to touch
>him, not because he
>   has no feeling but because he has so much.[8]

The first half of the conference thus was dominated by two efforts; first, the attempt to characterize individuality in several of its planes and dimensions, and second, the exploration of the problem of student unrest as an assertion of individuality.

With Professor Friedman's offering the conference took a distinctly tangential turn. He has always seen personal freedom as the supreme good, and he holds to the notion that most forms of government activity infringe on somebody's liberty. His paper, "The Market Versus the Bureaucrat," sought to explore the threats to freedom of action of the individual as visualized by the interaction of our national economy with certain government programs. Taking his cue from

---

[8] Marianne Moore, "The Student," in *What Are Years?* (New York: Macmillan, 1941).

Introduction

the expanded theme of the conference that scientific and technological advances create new forms of bondage that are grave threats to the integrity of the individual, Dr. Friedman started as an intellectual *provocateur,* with the disarming basic notion that the tyranny of man over man is the natural state of mankind! His thesis, however, was that in spite of this, our contemporary freedoms are truly remarkable, that there will always be threats, but that these will promote the correction of course and direction. Friedman's highly original and individualistic style of attack, recently described as a "mixture of supreme self-confidence and good humored needling,"[9] has made him a Peck's bad boy of economics.[10] It is in classical display through the wide convolutions of his highly readable argument. His final call is for an individual confrontation with government: ". . . we could achieve our objectives far better by using arrangements that give a greater scope to the market, that rely on 'participatory democracy' rather than on 'bureaucratic democracy.' "

Professor Lipset's paper, entitled "Prejudice and Politics in the American Past and Present," proves to be a fascinating, historical voyage through the ebb and flow of protest in our American political past. He identifies for us the early origins of political "backlash" and the reaction of dissenting groups since the beginning of our nation. He shows how early extremist appeals eventuate in a political movement or party when anxiety from social strain or decline in status lead to

[9] *Time* Magazine (19 December 1969), p. 71.
[10] *New York Times,* sec. VI, 25 January 1970.

DANIEL H. LABBY

feelings of deprivation; as models he considers two types of groups—"the never-hads" and the "once-hads." Professor Lipset analyzes their modes of action, procedure, and destiny in American life. In politico-historic perspective he gives us an overview of prejudice and bigotry throughout the evolution of our social and political life, with strong reference to religious and racist forces.

An electric moment developed in the symposium when René Dubos, the only natural scientist on the program, commented informally in beginning his remarks: "Nobody has yet mentioned what an individual is!" The audience reacted to this simple statement with loud applause. "My colleagues have been speaking of political man, social man, man in the abstract. I wish to speak of the man of flesh and bone." And in compelling style (beginning with the notion that "All human beings are related . . . but . . . the individuality of any person living now is different from that of anyone who has ever lived in the past or will live in the future. Each person is unique, unprecedented, and unrepeatable"), with elegance and wisdom, he drew the picture of biological man by calling on evidence from genetics and ecology, through expositions in evolution, and in free will versus determinism. In an extraordinary synthesis he rebuilt from many of the ideas in the symposium and insisted that man does not simply react to his environment but responds. "The chance in man's life comes from the creative responses that he and his societies make to the challenges of the total environment. To live is to respond and thereby to activate the mechanisms responsible for cre-

Introduction

ative adaptation." Dubos pointed out that in order to prosper, man demands a variety of opportunities for realization of his potentialities.

In the open discussion that followed, Dr. Dubos warned against tampering with the genetic endowment of man but emphasized the importance of dealing with the forces that shape the human mind, especially through maximizing the social environment to bring about improvement. He cited the fact that the brain of the child develops only in response to environmental stimulation and that early conditioning has been shown to be a powerful force in developing the immense range of human potential. On another occasion he had concluded: "Man has much freedom in selecting and creating his environment as well as his way of life and he determines by such decisions what he and his descendants will become. In this light man can truly 'make himself,' consciously and willfully. He has the privilege of responsible choice for his destiny—probably the noblest attribute of the human condition."[11]

It seemed an utter impossibility to summarize the astonishingly individual offerings of this wide-ranging conference by effectively combining their diverse elements. However, the memory of Dr. Kaplan's virtuosity in summarizing the first conference held everyone to his chair, despite fatigue and the late hour. What Kaplan offered was the final jewel in the setting, and he continued to polish it through the all-too-brief last moments before a fascinated audience. It revealed his

[11] Walton (ed.), *Today's Changing Society*.

DANIEL H. LABBY

extraordinary powers of synthesis and extemporaneous comment, the grasp and stretch of his mind, his love of learning, and his warmth and humor. Just as directed in his introduction, he "reached out" to everyone, and in concluding he charged us as individuals to "go our ways together."

Individuality and the New Society

Perspectives on the Theme

ABRAHAM KAPLAN

It is my task to put the theme of the conference into perspective. I take it that to put something into perspective means this: you begin with what would be quite clear if it were seen up close, and so contrive that it recedes into the distance, until at last it vanishes. If this understanding of my task is correct, I have some confidence that I shall be able to accomplish it.

I propose to use four guidelines toward that vanishing point. I shall first discuss the psychological aspects of individuality, then the social and the political aspects. Finally, when (as I anticipate) my time has been almost exhausted, I shall turn to the one area in which I can claim some professional competence—the moral or philosophical side of our subject.

The problem of individuality in our time is often posed in terms of a "numberized" society. There is no question that we are all of us individuals. But if to be an individual means only to be capable of being distinguished from others, then increasingly we are individuated these days by the many numbers associated with each of us—phone numbers, social security numbers, and so on. No doubt, before long some one number will be used for each person. These numbers provide for the individual, not an identity, but an identification—a way for him to be picked out from others, to be differentiated from them.

A century or so ago, a Hassidic master observed, "If I am I only because you are you, and you are you only because I am I, then I am not I and you are not you." Our identities—what we each feel so keenly within ourselves—cannot *consist* in these marks of identification, whether one or many. The psychological problem of individuality in our time begins with this, that though we are individuated, we are also depersonalized. I feel that I have not only been numbered, but that I am treated more and more as though I have *become* only a number, no longer a person.

Meeting as we are here under medical auspices, and with a strong cast in our discussions of interests deriving from the field of medicine, it is not inappropriate to note that for us laymen the medical profession often contributes to our sense of depersonalization. Not long ago, I participated in a staff seminar of a Department of Psychiatry. One of the psychiatric residents began his report: "The patient is a white male, age so-and-so. . . ." I sat thinking, "A white male what? A rabbit? A guinea pig?" That "the patient" was a human being, a young boy who had just gone through some agoniz-

Perspectives on the Theme

ing experiences, was an almost incidental fact of the case, brought into the discussion afterward, almost in passing.

Yet I could not blame the resident. He too is a human being, and the very nature of his medical training, I am afraid, leads him to feel that the ideal patient is the one on whom he learned his medicine—a corpse. The ideal patient is lifeless, inanimate, passive, altogether yielding. It has an identification—I shudder to imagine exactly how that is managed—but it has no identity.

So it is that many of us today feel that we have been robbed, are constantly being robbed, of our most precious essence, our innermost being as the particular human beings which we are. We are treated as identified individuals, but not as persons with identities.

The basic problem of individuality—in the strict sense in which I shall henceforth use the term: the identity of an individual person—the basic problem, as it seems to me with my own professional bias, does not stem from special features of the contemporary scene, but from circumstances intrinsic to the human condition. The problem arises from the very nature of the individual and of his relations to others, and it is this: if we move too close to others, we are in danger of losing our individuality; but if we keep ourselves too far from others, we face the danger that our individuality will no longer be worth keeping.

We struggle with this dilemma by moving alternately too close and too far away. When we are close, we feel that our individuality is threatened, that something precious is being taken away, or denied us; when we move away, we make our individuality secure, but at the price of loneliness, the price of feeling that no one understands us, no one knows us, no one loves us. Then each of us faces the really disturbing question, "Who do I myself think that I am?"

When we are close to others, we try to protect our individuality by acting on the principle that the best defense is a strong offense. We attack the individuality of the other, destroying him by swallowing him, accepting him only by first incorporating him into ourselves. These days this is called an expression of "the ecumenical spirit"; in more old-fashioned idioms, it is being "liberal," or being open to "pluralistic values." But we betray the premise on which we are really acting by defending our treatment of the others with the insistence that "After all, they're just like us." This implies that if they were not "just like us," if they were significantly different, we would be justified in—I do not know what. The point is that on this principle I preserve my individuality only at the expense of yours. If it is I who am on the receiving end of such "acceptance," I suffer from what we are calling today the problem of individuality in our time.

But I can also move away, withdraw from the other, and so neither swallow him nor be swallowed by him. The most common form of withdrawal is not "dropping out," but something less extreme, and perhaps for that very reason so much more widespread. It is apathy, indifference. A parent says to his teen-ager, "You know what the trouble is with you

Perspectives on the Theme

kids today? You're all so damned full of apathy! Do you know what that means?" The answer is, "No, and I couldn't care less!" This withdrawal today is as characteristic of the older generation as it is of the younger (perhaps they even learned it from us). We are quite adept at rationalizing our apathy, presenting it as one or another of a variety of admirable attitude and traits: sound judgment, good sense, reasonableness, prudence, and fair-mindedness. What these all come to is that we do not want to get involved, we do not want responsibility, we do not want commitment. But we do not want to be altogether out of it, either.

Consider that great myth of American liberalism, the so-called "independent voter." The myth is that while factionalists are inflamed with sectarian political passions, some few of us are men of philosophical detachment, of objectivity, of rationality; we examine all the evidence, weigh it dispassionately, and only then arrive at our conclusions. That is the fiction; the fact is (as I am sure Professor Lipset can attest, probably better than almost anyone else in the country) that every study of the "independent voter" has shown that he is the one who knows the least and cares the least about the political process. His so-called "independence" is more accurately described as indifference. Voting while indifferent may in turn be a symptom of struggling with the dilemma of being too close to the other or too far from him.

A final aspect of the psychological dimension of our theme which I wish to mention is the problem of achieving individuality within ourselves. Within each person are many selves, with only a sketchy awareness of one another, only a partial integration into a unity, perhaps even with significant conflicts among one another. As the sociologist Ernest Vandenhaag put it, our problem is not only that of the lonely crowd; the trouble is that many of us are crowded even when we are alone.

The word "individual" comes, after all, from the same root as the word "indivisible." It refers to something so unified that it cannot be separated without being destroyed. An individual is a multiplicity that works together in unity. But in this sense, individuality in the human being is an achievement, not something antecedently given. It is not something each of us had from the beginning, and still has except where it has been taken away by society, or by certain institutions, or by particular people. Individuality was not there from the beginning; in the fullest sense, indeed, it may not be there at all, except in the case of some very rare, fully integrated human beings.

I have no doubt that in the coming decades genetic engineering, organ transplantation, and related biotechnical skills will allow us to reshape the individual altogether, if we mean by the individual whatever differentiates an entity from others. We need also to develop new skills of education, new techniques of therapy, new patterns of living, it may be, which will allow us to reshape the *person,* the identity and not merely the identifications, so that we can progress toward the achievement of genuine individuality.

Although individuality has to do, tautologically, with the

Perspectives on the Theme

individual person, the problem of individuality cannot be formulated adequately without reference to the social situation in which alone an individual can become a person. It is the social situation which is chiefly responsible for the distress, if not downright despair, which most of us feel with regard to the problem of individuality. The trends seem to be such as to make the problem progressively worse.

The family used to be—or at least, so it seems to us—the locus of the most significant, most intense, and warmest human relationships; it is so no longer. Perhaps the family as a human grouping has outlived whatever usefulness it once had, just as the city as a pattern of social organization may have outlived its usefulness. At any rate, an increasingly large number of people behave as though this is what they believe about the family. The number of divorces rises steadily, and is a significant fraction each year of the number of marriages. What is involved here is not only a matter of quantity; if we had some way of measuring the *quality* of family life the situation might be seen to be even worse. For a family to stay together is not always a consummation devoutly to be wished; it might be better sometimes if the parties were put out of one another's reach.

In general, there seems to have been a loosening of social ties of all sorts. The need for others is no less than it ever was; we all feel this need keenly. But it seems that we can no longer rely on what once served to satisfy the need. Consider—as a symbol—what has happened to the dance in America. There was a time when dances were communal affairs—the western square dance, the Virginia reel, the round dances of the Old Country folk cultures. The dance was something enjoyed by the group as a whole. Then came the period of the couple dance. A group was present, but only as background to the involvement with one's own partner—sometimes a very intimate involvement; I still remember learning the tango, and my astonishment at discovering how much was legal! But now the dance has become, as it were, a solo performance. One still invites a partner to dance, I suppose, but it is hard for me to understand why. Each person dances as though carrying a sign which reads, "Nolo Me Tangere!"—Touch Me Not! Even eye contact is avoided. The human relation has become so subtle and indirect that there is a real question whether it exists at all.

I suppose it is inevitable that we respond to such changes in culture patterns as we do to new styles in art—with bewilderment, suspicion, and even hostility. No doubt human contact persists whatever the dance form. Yet what is symbolized by these changes in style seems to me more real than can be accounted for by the distortions of memory or the rigidity of old age. I am convinced that the increasing psychic distance which separates us from one another is more than a generation gap.

In fact, what happens between people more and more often today is something much more distressing than withdrawal. There is an increasing acceptance of violence as a style of relating to others. In *Peanuts* this point has been made as effectively, I think, as it can be. Linus is talking

Perspectives on the Theme

about a little girl who has moved in down the street, and says something like this: "I was watching her move in, and she came up to me and asked me if I wanted to be friends. I didn't know what to say—so I slugged her!"

There is a modern myth of a man walking along the high stone wall of an orphanage. He stumbles over a rock and finds a note tied to it. The note reads, "Whoever finds this—I love you!" The pathos of this image lies not only in its expression of a need *to* love, which may be greater even than the need to *be* loved. It lies also in the symbol. Each of us, living unloved behind our own walls, sends out the message over and over; we throw the rock, and often forget to tie the message to it. We know what to say—as Linus also does, to be sure. But we cannot bring ourselves to say it, and slug her instead.

Perhaps the most serious of the problems of individuality, looked at in social terms, is that society apparently is prepared fully to accept as individuals a smaller and smaller number of people. I do not want to play the numbers game with ages: I am not sure whether people are not to be trusted if they are over or under thirty or forty or sixty-five or twenty-one or what. The point is that society as a whole is denying individuality to greater and greater groups of people at both ends of the age distribution.

Young people today—whatever the cut-off point defining "young"—are subjected, it seems to me, to unprecedented (and I would think, unbearable) pressures. Granted that they have unprecedented opportunities, for which we at one time would have been very grateful. It remains true that we also deny much to the young, without regard to their qualifications. (Nowadays youth does not even lack—experience!) Increasingly we are saying to them, "You are not yet ready for the world of adult responsibility," when what we mean may be closer to this, "My adult world is not yet ready for the likes of you." In many colleges students are protesting that they do not want the college to stand *in loco parentis*. The irony is that the discipline being imposed in the academy is often more severe than what the student was subjected to at home. The college may be taking the place of a parent the student never had and does not want.

We do something similar in what we deny to the old as well. The proportion of Americans over sixty-five has virtually doubled in one generation; we can expect this proportion to increase as medical care becomes more effective and especially more widely available. But we are steadily lowering retirement ages, just as we are steadily increasing the number of years of schooling, training, and apprenticeship that must be served before a person is assigned unconditional responsibilities. We say to those we define as "old"—without regard to their qualifications, just as we disregard qualifications of the young—"You are no good to us any longer, but we are grateful to you. We want you to find a nice place to sit in the sun, with other useless people. But don't get in the way of those of us who are still doing the world's work." Yet the most desperate of human needs may be the need to be needed. Individuality surely cannot arise, to say nothing of its

Perspectives on the Theme

flourishing, unless that need is met, at least to some degree. I question whether society is in fact meeting the need.

Here also, as was true with regard to the psychological aspects of the matter, the problem cannot be attributed altogether to certain features of the present condition of man. Something intrinsic to the human situation enters into the difficulty. Social organization in its very nature confronts the individual with a dilemma. There is much action that an individual cannot undertake except jointly with others; yet in every joint enterprise new values, new goals impose themselves on the old ones, distort them, perhaps even supersede them.

Here is a simple, concrete example. It is my firm conviction that one of the most pernicious influences in American life today is advertising. Its progressive invasion of privacy, corrosion of taste, and perversion of value are far from irrelevant to the whole matter of individuality with which we are here concerned. Now, many people no doubt feel just as I do. If only we could get together and do something about it. How shall we proceed? Why, by collecting contributions to pay for a full-page ad in the *New York Times!* There is the dilemma.

Whenever we organize, the purposes we initially meant to serve become part of what is at stake in the organization. We cannot know what we will win—or lose—until the game has been played out. All we can be sure of is that we are running a risk. In every organization, among the most significant of the risks is depersonalization, of just the sort I was discussing at the beginning. Every organization must have policies, rules, operating procedures. It is in the very nature of such norms that they apply to cases without regard to the individual—an exception "proves" the rule only in the sense of testing it, not in the sense of demonstrating it. (All that the exception demonstrates is that it was not really a rule.) That the law is no respecter of persons is essential to its being law. Bureaucracy is not a degenerate form of administration; it is the nature of the beast. In today's multiversity it is not only the students who feel that they are not being treated as human beings. I wish that attention would sometimes be paid to the depersonalization and dehumanization of the faculty, and I have no doubt whatever that administrators can also make the same complaint, with equal justice. There is always a challenge to individuality, an inevitable loss of individuality in some measure, whenever an enterprise is sufficiently complex to require the coordinated efforts of a large group of human beings—say, any group with more than two or three individual members.

There are some political aspects of the problem which must also be looked at. It is tempting to suppose that here the problem takes on a new character. Granted that, human nature being what it is, social organization being what *it* is, there are some threats to individuality which we must just learn to live with. But on the political side, it seems as though certain people are deliberately doing something to our individuality; we don't like it, and we must fight back.

The point is, however, that the domain of political action

Perspectives on the Theme

is itself one of the loci of increasing depersonalization and dehumanization. Consider the difference between the old-time political machine and the contemporary political organization or "team." The Boss's followers were used to seeing him in the flesh (he usually had a great deal of it, too). He recognized you, knew you by name and much else besides, without a computerized memory to provide him with the information. He knew when your brother-in-law was going to need another job, and probably provided one, and got you the immigrant's visa for your uncle. Today, the political leader [*sic*] is seen remotely, only through the media. He is not a person, but an "image," and to him you are not even that, but only a vote or, at best, a constituent. We may think of him, and his wife even, by their first names; but the implied intimacy is empty and deceives no one, least of all ourselves.

We are alienated from power even in a democracy, perhaps even more when democratic symbols constantly raise expectations of being taken seriously as the persons we are, and the realities of the political situation constantly frustrate them. We admire the Englishman who wrote an indignant letter of complaint to some official and signed it, "You remain, Sir, my obedient servant. . . ." But alas, for most of us, our experience is that such a phrase is only a manner of speaking.

The question this raises is how far we, in turn, are obligated—legally or morally—to obey our servants. We are all exercised these days with determining the place of dissent and disobedience in a society in which so much power is being exercised over individuals by those who seem to have no regard for human individuality, whether in their own persons or in others.

I believe that any discussion of individuality in America today must re-emphasize how basic to democracy is the right of dissent. Individuality cannot survive if it cannot express itself. The individual must be able to call attention to his grievances, and to assert his individuality against whatever orthodoxy or consensus he might face.

Democratic theory has always had a moral basis, from Thomas Aquinas, Hugo Grotius, John Locke, and Thomas Jefferson to contemporary political philosophers. There has always been a reference to some law other than the law of the state—divine law, "natural law," the claims of conscience, and the like. Democracy has always enjoined a higher loyalty than that embodied in the morally dubious principle, "My country, right or wrong!" Here is another dilemma. On the one hand, in this perspective morality stands above the law of the state. But on the other hand, if each individual is given a personal veto over every act of the state, there is no such thing as a rule of law at all.

I might go even further. The moral law presents itself to each of us, after all, in ways conditioned by our own moral perceptions. Even if it is divine in origin, we can do what is right at best only as God gives us to see the right. The trouble is that He does not give it to all of us in the same way. There is a tyranny of conscience which can be quite as

Perspectives on the Theme

authoritarian and dehumanizing as the political tyranny it sees itself as opposing. Consider, for example, a parent whose conscience prevents him from allowing his children to be inoculated against diphtheria, say. Many children in the United States die for no other reason than that some parents take what they regard as a moral stand against inoculations. For my part, I do not feel that individual conscience is deserving of that much respect.

There is another difficulty with an absolutistic insistence on the rights of the individual. It is that dissent may become transformed into its own opposite, denying individuality to others and instead forcing upon them the dissenting view. This is something called *resistance,* but it is much more than a defense of one's own rights.

The determination of the individual to disobey a law which conflicts with his own moral perceptions has played an important part in our history and is playing perhaps an even more important part today. Disobedience on this basis can serve to revitalize values, to give them new meaning in terms of new conditions. But it can do so only if it is a *civil* disobedience—that is, only if it takes place within a framework of legality, if it acknowledges the basic values of the society, and aims at specific and limited objectives. When its goal is the transvaluation of all values, in a perspective which repudiates accepted social patterns, it becomes self-defeating. It purports to aim at changing certain laws while in fact operating to destroy the rule of law altogether.

The right of dissent is essential to individuality, and disobedience, if civil, may be necessary to protect it; resistance, however, destroys individuality. Here one is no longer protesting to express himself, to make his own commitment. Resistance is the attempt to coerce the decisions of another. It is one thing to let it be known where you stand; it is quite another to make it impossible for anyone else to take *his* stand anywhere except where you are willing for him to stand. Here both individuality and community have been repudiated. This repudiation betrays itself in that whereas dissent and even disobedience are usually associated with love for others, care for them, concern for their welfare, resistance is usually associated with hate, and rationalizes destroying the other. It invites and contributes to the violence it purports to condemn.

This brings me to the final aspect of the theme of individuality to which I would direct attention—the moral dimension. In our Judaeo-Christian tradition, we have long been accustomed to viewing morality as essentially a matter of the individual's obligations and responsibilities. The Hebrew prophets and their Christian successors emphasized the moral principles of an individual rather than a tribal ethic. Children are not to be punished for the sins of their fathers, nor any man for the failings of his fellows. A person is morally accountable only for what he himself does.

But here we are caught up in yet another dilemma. Although only the individual can be a moral agent, most significant action today is performed not by individuals but by collectivities, such as states and corporations; in that case,

Perspectives on the Theme

where shall we localize moral responsibility? Some people seek to escape the dilemma by turning their backs on collective action altogether, the tactic of "dropping out." But the notion that in this way moral responsibility is preserved is a pernicious rationalization of *ir*responsibility. In fact, as things are in the world today, effective action cannot be undertaken by an individual except in concert with other individuals. How moral responsibility is to be assigned to men engaged in collective action remains a real problem.

It may be that the very concept of individuality must undergo transformation, so that the collectivization, as it were, of both action and conscience will not be seen as antithetical to individuality but as helping to constitute it. To take a concrete example, there is much concern today about crime on our city streets. This is a real problem and I do not mean to belittle it, but I would like to draw more attention to the circumstance that the crimes are often committed in full view of people who do not help, do not summon help, do not even come forward afterward to give evidence, because as they say, "I don't want to get involved." When I speak about transforming the concept of individuality, I mean freeing the concept from such moral isolationism. The "I" that does not want to get involved is something less than an individual. If an individual is what has an identity and not just an identification, a personality and not merely a complex of data to be fed into a computer, it is not isolated from others but open to them, not encapsulated, but sharing common concerns—in a word, *involved*.

I am saying that the more we are involved with others the more of an individual we become. As the range of our fellow-feeling contracts, the boundaries of the self close in, and become at last the walls of a prison. As we withdraw from the problems of the aged, the young, the Negro, the poor, from suffering humanity in Vietnam or in any other part of the world, it is our own individualities that shrink. If anything human is foreign to me, I am myself, by just so much, less human. I believe it to be a fact of man's make-up and not merely a preachment of morality that I am indeed my brother's keeper; the voice of my brother's blood cries out to me from the ground because, in the most significant sense, his blood is my very own.

It is the predicament, the opportunity, and the glory of every man that he becomes an individual only as he reaches out to the rest of mankind.

Dissenting Youth and the New Society

KENNETH KENISTON

OF ALL groups in American society, youth will have to deal with the problem of individuality in the new society for the longest period. And as if in recognition of this fact, it is among American youth that the most vehement dissent against and alienation from our society are to be found. By examining the style of dissenting youth, and by attempting to understand how that style is related to the history of the past decades, we may better understand both the impact of our society and the prospects for the future.

Over the past ten years, my major efforts have involved an attempt to understand the psychological, social, and historical position of talented college students. In the course of this study, I have interviewed groups of highly alienated undergraduates and highly committed undergraduates, student

This research was supported by a grant from the Foundations Fund for Research in Psychiatry.

drop-outs and student stay-ins, drug-users and non-drug-users, students who seek psychiatric help and those who would not be caught dead in the office of a psychiatrist or counselor. In the summer of 1967, I had the opportunity to study a group of young men and women who were the leaders of Vietnam Summer, a New Left organization that attempted to organize new groups to oppose American involvement in Southeast Asia. The young men and women I studied thought of themselves as radicals, a self-characterization that was confirmed by the fact that all of them had previously spent at least one year in full-time work in the New Left—in community organizing, peace work, civil rights work in the South, and so on. The topic of my study was the process by which these young people had come to think of themselves as radicals—an exploration of their political development, of their family life, of their fantasies, fears, and hopes. But as this study progressed, it became more and more evident to me that these highly principled young men and women could only be understood in the context of the history of the post-war world, of the new society. Their lives, perhaps to an even greater degree than the lives of most of their contemporaries, were built upon the history of the era in which they grew up. Similarly, I came to feel that in the style and life experience of this small and perhaps unrepresentative group of young radicals, one could see broader issues of psychological development that equally affect others of their generation.

In my remarks here, I will start by considering briefly

Dissenting Youth and the New Society

some of the major characteristics of the new society in which today's individualistic and reformist youth has grown up. Next, I will consider briefly what I will term the "post-modern style" as it is emerging among dissenting groups in America and abroad. Third, by way of explaining this style, I will consider the credibility gap that is yawning between the generations today. And finally, I will turn to what seems to me the crucial issue in understanding the outlooks of today's youth or, for that matter, in understanding the world we live in—the issue of violence.

THE PSYCHO-HISTORICAL IMPACT OF THE POST-WAR ERA

The average age of those I interviewed was twenty-three: they were born near the end of the Second World War, and their earliest memories usually date from the years just after the war. The parents of these young radicals were in turn born around the time of the First World War; their grandparents, almost without exception, were the products of the nineteenth century. These young radicals are, then, members of the first post-war generation, while their parents are members of the first generation truly to emerge from the Victorian Era. To understand what this means for their psychology, style, and ideology, we need to remind ourselves of how much has changed in the past two decades.

Perhaps the main characteristic of the post-war era has been the breakneck pace of change in virtually every area of life, thought, and social organization. The last two decades have been a time of "radical" and "revolutionary" world upheaval; and although the changes in American society have been less dramatic and violent, they have been equally thoroughgoing. The mere fact of social change, of the continual alteration of the physical, human, and intellectual environment, is itself a major determinant of the lives of this post-war generation. For now, consider some of the specific changes which have occurred.

Hanging over the lives of all men and women during the past decades has been the Bomb, and the terrifying possibilities of technological death which it summarizes and symbolizes. These include not only holocaustal destruction by thermonuclear blast and radiation, but the possibility of slower forms of technological death from deliberately destructive biochemical interventions in the human ecology. To be sure, the possibility of premature and unannounced death has always been a fearful constant in human life. What is new about technological death is not only that it is quantitatively more violent and destructive than any previously imagined human invention, but that it is mechanical, impersonal, automatic, and absurd. One well-intentioned man (who means no harm and is only following orders) can press a button and set in motion a chain of events which could mean the gruesome death of most of those now alive. This possibility has been a constant backdrop to the development of a whole generation, incorporated into their lives not only in childhood terrors of the Bomb, but in the routine experience of air raid drills in school, in constant exposure to discussion of

Dissenting Youth and the New Society

fallout shelters, ballistic missiles, and antimissile defenses, and sometimes in a compulsive fascination with and terror of the technology of destruction. There are relatively few young Americans who, upon hearing a distant explosion, seeing a bright flash, or hearing a far-away sound of jets overhead at night, have not wondered for a brief instant whether this might not be "It."

A second crucial change in the past two decades is the still incomplete process of decolonization, the revolutionary liberation of the oppressed, exploited, and largely nonwhite majority of the world. As seen through the early recollections of young white Americans, this issue involves Negro Americans. For most young Americans, involvement in the American version of the world-wide liberation of the oppressed began in childhood or adolescence, when they "naturally" identified with the efforts of young Negro students to demand dignity and respect, whether by witnessing the early sit-ins and freedom rides on television, participating vicariously in the Little Rock demonstrations, or rejoicing in the Supreme Court decision of 1954. Many young Americans have become directly or vicariously involved with the Civil Rights movement. And when they were called upon to fight against movements of national liberation in Southeast Asia, the reaction of at least some was to identify American intervention with the spirit of southern sheriffs and prejudiced northerners, and to side with the anticolonial, nationalistic, nonwhite forces of revolution in Vietnam, caring little whether or not these forces were Communist.

Still another development in advanced societies is what might be termed the technologization of life. Terms like "automation," "rationalization," and "bureaucratization" suggest the sociologist's analysis of these developments; concepts like "objectification," "depersonalization," and "massification" are the social critic's response to them. But no matter how we characterize or respond to these ideas, the trend of the last two decades is clearly apparent: increasing bigness in government, the military, education, weaponry, automobiles, and cities; increasingly complex and differentiated organization in all areas in American life; a steady growth in the automation and computerization of many activities and decisions once reserved, for better or for worse, for human beings.

Such trends have their personal effects. Some young radicals had witnessed their parents' effort to prosper or even survive in a society of growing complexity and organization, which made ever greater demands for highly developed technical skills. Many had felt in their secondary schools and colleges what largeness and bureaucratization can mean; almost without exception, they had struggled to avoid being a "number" and insisted upon being treated as individuals. Furthermore, they are members of a generation raised on the corrosive skepticism of *Mad* magazine, taught paradoxically by television to be skeptical of commercial claims, reared during their preadolescent and adolescent years in the era of "togetherness" which denied but did not conceal the rifts in American life. Thoughtful, articulate, and principled young

Dissenting Youth and the New Society

men and women, most of them taught from an early age that there was more to life than "success" and remuneration, and surrounded by a technology in which they saw frightening possibilities of impersonality, they began in late adolescence to challenge the impersonality, dehumanization, overorganization, and commercialization of American life.

Finally, these young men and women grew up in an era of uninterrupted and automatic affluence. For most young men and women of middle-class backgrounds, the fact of affluence has been simply taken for granted. Although one or two of those interviewed came from lower-middle-class homes and considered themselves "poor" during their childhoods, none ever had to worry about food, clothing, or adequate education, nor even about a television set, a family car, and a vacation every year. When the time came for them to consider adult commitments, the question of income, social status, upward mobility, or finding a job had virtually no relevance. And when they realized at some point in their youth that the affluence they took for granted had not been extended to all Americans, much less to the impoverished two-thirds of the world, they reacted with outrage and dismay. In an affluent era, radicals (who almost always come from the middle class) show less guilt and more outrage at poverty: they do not feel ashamed of their own prosperity, but angry at the system that still excludes others from a share in it.

Although the young radicals with whom I have been concerned possess a greater historical consciousness than most of their contemporaries, the historical ground on which they developed was to a large extent the same ground on which their entire generation, not only in America but throughout the world, also developed. In the modern world, there are, of course, vast and important cultural and national differences. Yet in other respects the experience of youth in all nations is becoming increasingly similar: the same historical events affect and shape all, and similar youth phenomena are apparent in a variety of nations, advanced and developing. Sometimes to greater and sometimes to lesser degree, the revolutions that have affected American youth have affected their contemporaries elsewhere. We are moving toward a world in which there is only one history—world history.

THE POST-MODERN STYLE

As I have emphasized, these young radicals are different from most of their contemporaries by virtue of their unusual psychological development, because of their commitment to the New Left, because of their unusual resonance with political events. The great majority of young Americans in their early twenties are not radicals, nor even dissenters, protesters, and activists, are not alienated hippies, bohemians, or beatniks. So it is only as a speculation that we can generalize from radical and dissenting youth to other youth, and then always with the proviso that we are speaking of a minority, which helps set the tone and style of its generation but constitutes only a small part of that age group.

Dissenting Youth and the New Society

In emphasizing "style" rather than ideology, identity, traits, objectives, or characteristics, I mean to suggest that the communalities in post-modern youth are to be found in the *way* in which they approach the world, rather than in their actual behavior, ideologies, or goals. Indeed, the focus upon "process" rather than program may be the central characteristic of the post-modern style, reflecting a world in which process and change are more obvious than purpose and goal. For as I will suggest, post-modern youth, at least in America, are themselves very much in process, unfinished in their development, deliberately open to an unpredictable future. In such a world, where ideologies come and go, and where revolutionary change is the rule, a "style," a *way* of doing things, is more possible to maintain than any more fixed goals or constancies of behavior.

In contemporary American society, the style of post-modern youth is best illustrated by the New Left and the hippies, informal youth groups which in their combined active membership constitute but a small percentage of their generation, although they are already giving a distinctive imprint to their contemporaries. There are many important differences between the hippie and the more activist radical, but beyond these, the two groups have in common a visible discomfort with existing American society, and an often agonized search for ways to change or escape this society. Moreover, both hippies and young radicals tend to be drawn from similar backgrounds: upper-middle-class, politically liberal, secular families, excellent educations, and attendance at prestigious colleges.

Fluidity of Identity

Post-modern youth displays a special personal and psychological openness, flexibility, and unfinishedness. Although I have spoken of the development of a "radical identity," the term "identity" suggests a greater fixity, stability, and "closure" than most young radicals in fact possess. Indeed, it seems possible that the traditional description of identity development may need to be changed to allow for the impact of social change upon elite youth. No longer is it possible to speak of the normal "resolution" of identity issues; and our earlier fear of the ominous implications of "prolonged adolescence" must now be qualified by an awareness that in post-modern youth many "adolescent" issues and qualities persist long past the time when in earlier eras they "should" have ended. Increasingly, the identity development of post-modern youth is tied to social and historical changes which have not occurred and which may never occur. Thus, psychological "closure," shutting doors and burning bridges, becomes impossible. The concept of the personal future and the "life work" are ever more hazily defined; the effort to change, redefine, or reform oneself does not cease with the arrival of biological adulthood.

This openness extends through all areas of life. Both hippie and New Left movements are nondogmatic, nonideological, and to a large extent hostile to doctrine and formula. In

Dissenting Youth and the New Society

the New Left, the focus is on "tactics"; among hippies, on simple direct acts of love and communication. In neither group does one find long-range plans, social and political programs, or life patterns laid out in advance. The vision of the personal and collective future is blurred and vague: later adulthood is left deliberately open. In neither group is psychological development considered complete; in both groups, identity, like history, is fluid and indeterminate. In one sense, of course, identity development takes place; but in another sense, identity is never finally achieved, but is always undergoing transformations that parallel the transformations of the historical world.

Generational Identification

Post-modern youth view themselves primarily as part of a generation rather than an organization; they identify with their contemporaries as a group, rather than with elders; and they do not have clearly defined leaders and heroes. Their deepest collective identification is to their own group or "movement"—a term that in its ambiguous meanings points not only to the fluidity of post-modern youth, but also to their physical mobility and the absence of traditional patterns of leadership and emulation. Among young radicals, for example, the absence of heroes or older leaders is impressive: even those five years older are sometimes viewed with mild amusement or suspicion. They live together in groups, but these groups are without clear leaders. And although post-modern youth are often widely read in the "literature" of the

New Left or consciousness-expansion, no one person or set of people is central to their intellectual beliefs. Generations today are separated by a very brief span; and the individual's own phase of youthful usefulness—for example, as hippie or organizer—is limited to a relatively few years. Generations come and go quickly; whatever is to be accomplished must therefore be done soon.

Generational consciousness also entails a feeling of psychological disconnection from previous generations. Among young radicals, there is a strong feeling that the older ideologies are exhausted or irrelevant, expressed in detached amusement at the doctrinaire disputes of the "Old Left" and impatience with "old liberals." Among hippies, the irrelevance of the parental past is even greater: if there is any source of insight, it is the timeless tradition of the East, not the values of the previous generation in American society. But in both groups, the central values are those created in the present by the "movement" itself.

Personalism

Both groups are highly personalistic in their styles of relationship. Among hippies, personalism usually entails privatism, a withdrawal from efforts to be involved in or change the wider social world; among young radicals, personalism is joined with efforts to change the world. But despite this difference, both groups care most deeply about the creation of intimate, loving, open, and trusting relationships within small groups of people. The ultimate judge of man's life is the quality of his personal relationship; the greatest sin—what sends people into psychotherapy—is to be unable to relate to others in a direct, face-to-face, one-to-one relationship.

The obverse of personalism is the discomfort created by any nonpersonal, "objectified," professionalized, and above all exploitative relationship. Manipulation, power relationships, super-ordination, control, and domination are at violent odds with the I-thou mystique. Failure to treat others as fully human is viewed with dismay in others and with guilt in oneself. Even with opponents the goal is to establish intimate confrontations in which the issues can be discussed openly.

Nonasceticism

Post-modern youth is nonascetic, expressive, and sexually free. The sexual openness of the hippie world has been much discussed and criticized in the mass media. One finds a similar sexual and expressive freedom among many young radicals, although it is less provocatively demonstrative. In the era of the pill, responsible sexual expression is more possible outside of marriage, at the same time that sexuality is less laden with guilt, fear, and prohibition. As asceticism disappears, so does promiscuity: the personalism of post-modern youth requires that sexual expression must occur in the context of "meaningful" human relationships of intimacy and mutuality. Marriage is increasingly seen as an institution for having children, but sexual relationships are viewed as the natural concomitant of close relationships between the sexes. What is important is not sexual activity itself, but the context in which it occurs. Sex is right and natural between people who are "good to each other," but sexual exploitation—failure to treat one's partner as a person—is strongly disapproved.

Antitechnologism

Post-modern youth has grave reservations about many of the technological aspects of the contemporary world. The depersonalization of life, commercialism, careerism, and familism, the bureaucratization and complex organization of advanced nations—all seem intolerable to these young men and women, who seek to create new forms of association and action to oppose the technologism of our day. Bigness, impersonality, stratification, and hierarchy are rejected, as is any involvement with the furtherance of technological values. In reaction to these values, post-modern youth seeks simplicity, naturalness, personhood, and even voluntary poverty.

But a revolt against technologism is only possible in a technological society; and to be effective, it must inevitably exploit technology to overcome technologism. Thus, in post-modern youth, the fruits of technology—synthetic hallucinogens in the hippie subculture, modern communications among young radicals—and the affluence made possible by technological society are a precondition for a post-modern style. The demonstrative poverty of the hippie would be meaningless in a society where poverty is routine; for the radical to work for subsistence wages as a matter of choice is

Dissenting Youth and the New Society

to *have* a choice not available in most parts of the world. Furthermore, to "organize" against the pernicious aspects of the technological era requires high skill in the use of modern technologies of organization: the long-distance telephone, the mass media, high-speed travel, and so on. In the end, then, it is not the material but the spiritual consequences of technology that post-modern youth opposes. What *is* adamantly rejected is the contamination of life by the values of technological organization and production. A comparable rejection of the psychological consequences of current technology, coupled with the simultaneous ability to exploit that technology, probably characterizes all dissenting groups in all epochs.

Participation

Post-modern youth is committed to a search for new forms of organization and action where decision making is collective, where arguments are resolved by "talking them out," and where self-examination, interpersonal criticism, and group decision making are fused. The objective is to create new styles of life that humanize rather than dehumanize, that activate and strengthen the participants rather than undermining or weakening them. And the primary vehicle for such participation is the small, face-to-face, primary group of peers.

This search can hardly be deemed successful as yet, especially in the New Left, where effectiveness in the wider social and political scene remains to be demonstrated. But there may yet evolve from the hippie "tribes," small Digger communities, and primary groups of the New Left new forms of association in which self-criticism, awareness of group interaction, and the accomplishment of social and political goals go hand in hand. The effort to create groups in which individuals grow from their participation in the group extends far beyond the New Left and the hippie world; the same search is seen in the widespread enthusiasm for "sensitivity training" groups and even in the increasing use of groups as a therapeutic instrument. Nor is this solely an American search: one sees a similar focus, for example, in the Communist nations, with their emphasis on small groups which engage in the "struggle" of mutual criticism and self-criticism.

The search for effectiveness combined with participation has also led to the evolution of "new" forms of social and political action. The newness of such tactics as parades and demonstrations is open to some question; perhaps what is new is the style in which old forms of social action are carried out. The most consistent effort is to force the opponent into a personal confrontation with one's own point of view. Sit-ins, freedom rides, insistence upon discussions, silent and nonviolent demonstrations, and confrontations—all have a prime objective to "get through to" the other side, to force reflection, to bear witness as an existential act, and to impress upon others the sincerity and validity of one's own principles. There is much that is old and familiar about this.

Yet the underlying purpose of many of the emerging forms of social and political action—whether they are "human be-ins," "love-ins," peace marches, confrontations, resistance, or "teach-ins"—has a new flavor: the hope that by expressing his own principles, by "demonstrating" his convictions, the young demonstrator can lure his opponents into participating with his own values.

Antiacademicism

Among post-modern youth, one finds a virtually unanimous rejection of the "merely academic." This rejection is a manifestation of a wider insistence on the relevance, applicability, and personal meaningfulness of knowledge. It would be wrong simply to label the trend "anti-intellectual," for most new radicals and some hippies are themselves highly intellectual people. What *is* demanded is that intelligence be engaged with the world, just as action should be informed by knowledge.

To post-modern youth, much of what is taught in schools, colleges, and universities is largely irrelevant to living in the last third of the twentieth century. Some academics are seen as indirect apologists for the organized system in the United States. Much of what the academics teach is considered to be simply unconnected to the experience of post-modern youth. They seek new ways of learning: ways that combine action with reflection, ways that fuse engagement in the world with understanding of it. In an era of rapid change, the accrued wisdom of the past is cast into question, and youth seeks not only new knowledge, but new ways of arriving at knowledge.

Nonviolence

Finally, post-modern youth of all persuasions meet on the ground of nonviolence. For hippies, the avoidance of and calming of violence is a central objective, symbolized by gifts of flowers to policemen and the slogan, "Make love, not war." And although nonviolence as a philosophical principle has lost most of its power in the New Left, nonviolence as a psychological orientation is a crucial—perhaps *the* crucial—issue. The nonviolence of post-modern youth should not be confused with pacifism: these are not necessarily young men and women who believe in turning the other cheek or who are systematically opposed to fighting for what they believe in. But the basic style of both radicals and hippies is profoundly opposed to warfare, destruction, and exploitation of man by man, and to violence whether on an interpersonal or an international scale.

THE CREDIBILITY GAP: PRINCIPLE AND PRACTICE

In considering the historical context for the development of post-modern youth, I have emphasized the massive and violent social changes of the past two decades. During this era of rapid social change the values most deeply internalized in the members of the parental generation and expressed in their behavior in time of crisis are frequently very different from the more "modern" principles, ideals, and values which they have professed and attempted to practice in bringing up their children. Filial perception of the discrepancy between practice and principle may help explain the special sensitivity among post-modern youth to the "hypocrisy" of the previous generation.

The grandparents of today's twenty-year-olds were generally born at the end of the nineteenth century and brought up during the pre-World War I years. Heirs of a Victorian tradition as yet unaffected by the value revolutions of the twentieth century, they reared their children (the parents of today's youth) in families that emphasized respect, the control of impulse, obedience to authority, and the traditional "inner-directed" values of hard work, deferred gratification, and self-restraint.

During their lifetimes, however, these parents of post-modern youth (and in particular the most intelligent and advantaged among them) were exposed to a great variety of new values which often changed their nominal faiths. During their youth in the 1920s and 1930s, older Victorian values were challenged, attacked, and all but discredited, especially in educated middle-class families. Young men and women who went to college during this period (as did most of the parents of those who can be termed "post-modern" today) were influenced outside their families by a variety of "progressive," "liberal," and even psychoanalytic ideas that contrasted sharply with the values of their childhood families. Moreover, during the 1930s, many of the parents of today's upper-middle-class youth were exposed to or involved with the ideals of the New Deal, and sometimes to more radical interpretations of man, society, and history. Finally, in the 1940s and 1950s, when it came time to rear their own children, the parents of today's elite youth were strongly influenced by "permissive" views of child rearing that again contrasted sharply with the techniques by which they themselves had been raised. Thus, many middle-class parents moved during their lifetimes from the Victorian ethos in which they had been socialized to the less moralistic, more humanitarian, and more "expressive" values of their own adulthoods.

But major changes in values, when they occur in adult life, are likely to be far from complete. To have grown up in a family where unquestioning obedience to parents was expected, but to rear one's own children in an atmosphere of "democratic" permissiveness and self-determination—and never to revert to the practices of one's own childhood—requires a change of values more total and comprehensive than most adults can achieve. Furthermore, behavior which springs from values acquired in adulthood often appears somewhat forced, artificial, or insincere to the sensitive observer. Children, clearly the most sensitive observers of their own parents, are likely to sense a discrepancy between their parents' avowed and consciously held values and their "basic instincts" with regard to child rearing. Furthermore, the parental tendency to "revert to form" is greatest in times of family crisis, which are the times that have the weightiest effect upon children.

In a time of rapid social change, then, a special "credibility gap" is likely to open between the generations. Children are apt to perceive a considerable discrepancy between what the parents avow as their values and the actual assumptions from which parental behavior springs. In the young radicals interviewed, for example, the focal issue of adolescent rebellion against parents seems to have been just this discrepancy: the children arguing that their parents' endorsement of independence and self-determination for their children was "hypocritical" in that it did not correspond with the real behavior of the parents when their children actually sought independence. Similar perceptions of "hypocrisy" occurred for others around racial matters: for example, there were a few parents who in principle supported racial and religious equality, but who became violently upset when their children dated someone from another race or religion.

Of course, no society ever fully lives up to its own professed ideals. There is always a gap between creedal values and actual practices, and the recognition of this gap constitutes a powerful motive for social change. But in most societies, especially when social change is slow and institutions are powerful and unchanging, there occurs what we might term the "institutionalization of hypocrisy." Children and adolescents routinely learn when it is "reasonable" to expect that the values people profess will be implemented in their behavior, and when it is not reasonable. There develops an elaborate system of commentary upon the society's creedal values, excluding certain people or situations from the full weight of these values or "demonstrating" that apparent inconsistencies are not really inconsistencies at all. Thus, in almost all societies, a "sincere" man who "honestly" believes one set of values is frequently allowed to ignore them completely—for example, in the practice of his business, in many interpersonal relationships, in dealings with foreigners, in relationships with his children, and so on—all because these areas have been officially defined as exempt from the application of his creedal values.

In a time of rapid social change and value change, however, the institutionalization of hypocrisy seems to break down. "New" values have been in existence for so brief a period that the exemptions to them have not yet been defined, the situations to be excluded have not yet been determined, and the universal gap between principle and practice appears in all of its nakedness. The mere fact of a discrepancy between social values and social practice is not unusual. But what is special about the present situation of rapid value change is, first, that parents themselves tend to have two conflicting sets of values, one related to the experience of their early childhood, the other to the ideologies and principles acquired in adulthood; and second, that no stable institutions or rules for defining hypocrisy out of existence have yet been fully evolved. In such a situation, children see the Emperor's nakedness with special clarity, recognizing the

Dissenting Youth and the New Society

value conflict within their parents and perceiving the hypocritical gap between creed and behavior.

This points to one of the central characteristics of post-modern youth: they insist on taking seriously a great variety of political, personal, and social principles which "no one in his right mind" ever before thought of extending to dealings with strangers, relations between the races, or international politics. For example, peaceable openness has long been a creedal virtue in our society, but it has never been extended to foreigners, particularly those with dark skins. Similarly, equality has long been preached, but the "American dilemma" has been resolved by a series of institutionalized hypocrisies which exempted Negroes from the application of this principle. Love has always been a central value in Christian society, but really to love one's enemies—to be generous to policemen, customers, criminals, servants, or foreigners—has been considered folly.

These speculations on the credibility gap between the generations in a time of rapid change may help explain two crucial facts about post-modern youth: first, they frequently come from highly principled families with whose principles they continue to agree; second, they have the outrageous temerity to insist that individuals and societies live by the values they preach.

VIOLENCE: SADISM AND CATACLYSM

The issue of violence is central not only for young radicals, but for post-modern youth the world over. Recall, once again, some of the early memories of the young radicals interviewed: the destructiveness of the atomic bomb; a tank grinding over the rubble of war; a man escaping from a menacing mob; striking this man in the face; the exploitation of the darker-skinned by the white. In all of these memories, issues of violence are central; in each of them, violence without finds echo and counterpart in the violence of inner feelings. The term "violence" suggests both of these possibilities: the *psychological* violence of sadism, exploitation, and aggression; and the *historical* violence of war, cataclysm, and holocaust. In the lives of young radicals, as of most of their generation, the threats of inner and outer violence are fused, each activating, exciting, and potentiating the other. To summarize a complex thesis into a few words: *the issue of violence is to this generation what the issue of sex was to the Victorian world.*

Stated differently, what is most deeply repressed, rejected, feared, controlled, and projected onto others by the postmodern generation is no longer their own sexuality. Sex, for most of this generation, is much freer, more open, less guilt- and anxiety-ridden. But violence, whether in oneself or in others, has assumed new prominence as the prime source of inner and outer terror. That this should be so in the modern world is readily understandable. Over all of us hangs the continual threat of a technological violence more meaningless, absurd, premature, total, and unpremeditated than any ever imagined before. I have stressed the resonance of individual life with historical change, emphasizing that history is not merely the backdrop for human development, but its ground. To be grounded in the history of the past two decades is to have stood upon, to have lived amidst, to have experienced both directly and vicariously, violent upheaval, violent world-wide revolution, and the unrelenting possibility of world-wide destruction. To have been alive and aware in America during the past decade has been to be exposed to the assassination of a president and the televised murder of his alleged murderer, to the well-publicized slaughter of Americans by their mad fellow countrymen, and to the recent violence in our cities. To have been a middle-class child in the past two decades is to have watched daily the violence of television, both as it reports the bloodshed and turmoil of the American and non-American world, and as it skillfully elaborates and externalizes in repetitive dramas the potential for violence within each of us.

It therefore requires no assumption of an increase in biological aggressivity to account for the salience of the issue of violence for post-modern youth. The capacity for rage, spite, and aggression is part of our endowment as human beings: it is a constant potential of human nature. But during the past two decades—indeed, starting before the Second World War—we have witnessed violence on a scale more frightening than ever before. Like the angry child who fears that his rage alone will destroy those around him, we have become vastly more sensitive to and fearful of our inner angers, for we live in a world where even the mildest irritation, multiplied a billionfold by modern technology, might destroy all civilization. The fact of violent upheaval and the possibility of cataclysm has been literally brought into our living rooms during the past twenty years: it has been interwoven with the development of a whole generation. For these young radicals, as for many others of their generation, the issue of violence, inner and outer, has probably been *the* central unifying theme in their lives.

I have already discussed many of the themes and tensions —psychological, interpersonal, and organizational—that are related to the issue of violence. The avoidance, elimination, and control of violence, whether in the form of warfare, naked aggression, or exploitation of others, is a central goal and psychological orientation of the New Left. Indeed, some of the special dilemmas of the New Left seem related to the zealous and systematic effort to avoid any action or relationship in which inner or outer violence may be evoked. Recall, for example, the consistent efforts made to avoid domination within the movement, and to eliminate all manipulation in the world at large. Recall, too, the distrust of authority, the avoidance of leadership lest it lead to domination, the hostility to "flashiness" in political activities lest it lead to exploitation. Remember, finally, the deliberate efforts of many young radicals to overcome their own angers and aggressions, their remarkable ability to retain control when provoked, their basic preference for "nonviolent" forms of protest and action, and their largely successful struggle to overcome in themselves any conscious vestige of exploitation, aggression, or manipulation in human relations.

Dissenting Youth and the New Society

I do not mean to suggest that young radicals in particular or post-modern youth in general are tight-lipped pacifists, rage-filled deniers of their own inner angers. On the contrary, exuberance, passion, and zest are the rule rather than the exception. Nor are young radicals incapable of anger, rage, and resentment, especially when their principles are violated. But perhaps more than most, they learned early in their lives the fruitlessness of conflict; and this lesson, in later years, was among the many intertwined forces that went into their decisions to work for Vietnam Summer.

In young radicals, as in many of their generation, the avoidance of violence is central. Among the goals of the New Left, the end of warfare, exploitation, and domination is central. Within the movement itself, the search for new forms of social organization and political action that avoid manipulation, oppression, and control is crucial. Within young radicals themselves, the struggle to overcome their tendencies to anger, rage, and destructiveness constitutes a unifying theme. In this last endeavor, the young men and women whom I interviewed had been largely successful, probably because whatever inner disposition to violence they possessed has been channeled into "aggressive" efforts to create outlooks and institutions that would bring an end to violence.

In pointing to the psychological dimension of the issue of violence, I do not mean to attribute causal primacy either to the experiences of early life or to their residues in adulthood. My thesis is rather that for those members of this generation who possess the greatest historical awareness, the psychological and historical possibilities of violence have come to potentiate each other, producing a new emphasis on the sanctity of life. To repeat: witnessing the acting out of violence on a scale more gigantic than ever before, or imaginatively participating in the possibility of world-wide holocaust activates the fear of one's own violence; heightened awareness of one's inner potential for rage, anger, or destructiveness increases one's sensitivity to the possibility of violence in the world.

This same process of historical activation of inner violence has occurred, I believe, throughout the modern world, and brings with it not only the intensified efforts to curb violence that we see in this small segment of post-modern youth, but other more frightening possibilities. These young radicals, to an unusual degree, remain open to and aware of their own angers and aggressions, and this awareness creates in them a sufficient understanding of inner violence to enable them to control it in themselves and oppose it in others. Most men and women, young or old, possess less insight: their inner sadism is projected onto others whom they thereafter loathe or abjectly serve; or, more disastrously, historically heightened inner violence is translated into outer aggression and murderousness, sanctioned by self-righteousness.

Thus, if the issue of violence plagues post-modern youth, it is not because these young men and women are more deeply enraged than most. On the contrary, it is because they have been forced to confront this issue more squarely in themselves and in the world than have any but a handful of their fellows. If they have not yet found solutions, they have at least faced an issue so dangerous that most of us find it too painful even to acknowledge, and they have done so, most remarkably, without identifying with that which they oppose. And their still incomplete lives and unfinished work pose for us all the crucial question upon which our survival as individuals and as a world depends: can we create new forms to control historical and psychological violence before their fusion destroys us all?

Present Discontents of the Student Age Group

LIONEL ROBBINS

My ASSIGNMENT in this symposium is to discuss the causes and the validity of current manifestations of unrest and rebellion among the young. I shall assume that this covers both the concrete complaints and demands of the movement for student power and the wider grievances and moods of which this movement is perhaps largely an accidental by-product; and I shall divide my remarks accordingly.

At the outset, however, I should like to make explicit certain cautions. The subject is highly complex and the sort of generalization which is necessarily involved in any treatment in short compass is liable to oversimplification. This will not lead me to shirk generalization, but I should hope that what I say will be taken in the context of these preliminary warnings.

First I think we should beware of treating the problem as if it were altogether new. I shall be arguing toward the end

Present Discontents of the Student Age Group

of my remarks that there is indeed a new and alarming element in the underlying causes of the present situation. But it would be a mistake to treat much of what is happening today as if it were an entirely novel appearance in history. I personally can remember similar manifestations in the interwar period; and the part played by students in shaking the authority of governments in many areas and at many times has long been recognized. As I was preparing this paper, I happened to be rereading Turgenev's masterpiece *Fathers and Sons,* written more than a hundred years ago; it deals with just this problem of alienation and revolt among the younger generation. Indeed, I am inclined to argue that there are profound psychological reasons why this should be a more or less permanent feature of the human situation. Bernard Shaw once said that every man over forty is a scoundrel. I believed this to be true before I was forty; and now I am long past that age, I know it to be true introspectively. What he meant, of course, was that as life goes on a man comes to live with all sorts of abuses and imperfections which, viewed in the abstract or with eyes not yet reconciled to the business of making some terms with imperfect reality, are intrinsically provocative of hostility and quixotic action. I am not arguing that, given the limitations of life on this planet, such reactions are always sensible or productive of good results. I am only arguing that, given these differences of attitude, some permanence of tension is only to be expected.

Second, I am inclined to think that, in any interpretive approach to particular manifestations, we may miss the practical solution if we concern ourselves too much with general causes. Granted that there are general causes operating, we nevertheless do violence to the facts if we do not recognize particular influences. I think for instance of the troubles at Berkeley and the London School of Economics, both of which I saw at close quarters—at Berkeley during a very short visit, at LSE, where I have taught the greater part of my life, during the whole dismal episode. Now it is true that student opinion at both centers was in an initially sensitive condition, apt to flare up if some provocative, or allegedly provocative, incident occurred. It is true too that there were common influences in the shape of common personalities— one of the leaders of the revolt at LSE came from Berkeley and another from Amherst, where he had been involved in similar agitations. But the occasion of the troubles differed markedly. I will not go into the complicated origins of the Berkeley episode. But they were certainly different from what happened at LSE, where the troubles began with accusations of racial prejudice against a director-elect, who in fact in earlier years had thrown up a promising academic career to succor and assist the victims of Hitler's persecution and who had devoted a good deal of the rest of his life to creating multiracial educational institutions in Africa. Whatever the rights and wrongs of what happened in California, there was nothing so shabby, so utterly vile as this. And I think that if one went into the causes of other student revolts in recent history, one would discover a marked diversity of specific causes, each of which would be adequate to explain a good deal of what took place in the individual instances concerned.

Having uttered these cautions, however, I hasten to say that I do not dispute what after all is the subject of this essay, that today there do exist among the student population and youth generally moods of unrest and antagonism which, while special to this day and age, probably have common causes. At any rate, they have given rise to common demands and common attitudes, and are susceptible at least to some common analysis. In approaching the subject, then, I shall deal first with specific movements and other grievances among the student population, and then with the wider causes of unrest among sensitive and intelligent youth generally.

I will begin with the movement for student power, the demand for the control or partial control by students of university institutions. This movement is indeed something new. I do not know of any earlier manifestation of this sort —at any rate in modern times. It assumes two forms, which we may call, respectively, the antirational and the rational. The one demands power as an end in itself, regardless of its compatibility with the other ends of the society; the other purports to provide a justification of its demands in terms of compatibility with, or indeed benefit to, social aims in general.

The antirational branch of this movement has much in common with the more extreme forms of the Syndicalist movement which flourished in Europe at the beginning of the century and which finds its classic formulation in the

Reflections on Violence of George Sorel, a work which in its day enjoyed a sort of snob prestige as an alleged liquidator of all traditional values. When it does not consist in a mere affirmation—"We want power and we mean to have it"—it is essentially an expression of contempt for or disgust at existing institutions. Democracy has failed—look at the present state of affairs. The existing structure of society is hateful. There is no hope of change through the normal channels of politics. There is nothing for it but for groups of dedicated persons to capture certain islands of possible autonomy and, obliterating all traces of an ignoble past, to govern them according to the heart's desire of the progressive and enlightened spirits who have emerged triumphant from the struggle. It is essentially a defiance of a coordinated society. It is no accident that it is sometimes associated with an admiration for violence as such which is essentially what society exists to eliminate.

Conceived in this spirit, the prospects of student power are not exactly hopeful. The prospects of any form of syndicalism never were. The intellectual *coup de grâce* was administered long ago by the wisecrack of the Webbs—the sewers for the sewage men. In the United Kingdom, the majority of the students receive not only their fees but also their day-to-day maintenance from the central government or the local authorities. In such circumstances the claim that they should run the institutions intended for their instruction, without any ultimate control from teachers and the outside world, is not likely to command wide acceptance. And even in less egalitarian atmospheres, where students or their parents make more sacrifice to finance their education, it is not very probable that the trusts or the civic authorities responsible for the buildings and apparatus of university life will be prepared to surrender control to a mere gesture of defiance, however vehement and explosive. And since the rebels are a minority—and generally a small minority even of the student body—there can be little doubt who will eventually win.

Confronted with this brute fact, most members of this group are usually prepared to beat a strategic retreat into the camp of those who are prepared to use reason and persuasion and who base their demands for student control or extensive student representation, not on some wild nihilist gesture, but upon arguments designed to show that social interest and social equity would be best secured thereby. And since, in my judgment, there is at least an infusion of cogency in some of these arguments, it is certainly worth while devoting more time to their examination.

Let me say at once that I recognize justice and utility in the claim that students should be consulted in some way or other in matters in which their direct convenience and interest are clearly concerned; it may be taken as an axiom that university administrators and senates are not omniscient. There arise continually positions in which their regulations and directives may cause needless inconvenience or even hardship to students. And there is everything to be said for forms of organization which permit student opinion on such matters to be regularly ventilated, rather than leaving its emergence to chance conversation or *ad hoc* demonstrations against particular grievances. Where university authorities resist the establishment of any organization of this sort, they have only themselves to thank if the reaction sometimes takes an ugly form.

How exactly such organizations should be constituted is a matter about which opinions may differ and in regard to which local tradition and social custom may well play a determining part. The obvious form is student representation on the various committees that deal with the administrative functions concerned—library committees, refectory committees, entertainment committees, and so on, taking for granted a good deal of student autonomy in regard to sport and athletics. But if it serves to reassure the student body that the more general aspects of policy are considered with due regard to their welfare, I see no objection in principle to some limited representation on the main organs of government, always subject to the reservation that where questions of staff appointments and examinations are concerned, the student element is excluded. I should make this concession with no great hope that it would bring any advantage other than the relief of tension. But I should not oppose cautious experimentation.

Beyond this, I see serious difficulties. The idea that the functioning of universities as such, the appointment of academic staff and officers, the setting of standards, the advancement of knowledge, are likely to be benefited by student control does not seem to me plausible. On the contrary, I see in this idea grave dangers to the very purposes for which universities are founded; and although always anxious to proceed by persuasion rather than by standing on one's rights, in the end, I should be prepared to resist it without concessions.

Why is this? I examine my conscience carefully in this respect, and I am clear enough that it does not arise from any feelings of antagonism or superiority to students in general. Personally, I love students and find their outlook and their company often vastly more congenial than that of many of my colleagues. But fundamentally I take what may be called the functional view of such matters—power should rest with those who best discharge the particular functions involved. And, as I see things, judgment on the suitability of appointments and degree requirements is not among the functions which students, *as students,* are well fitted to perform. If they were, if they were competent to gauge academic quality or to determine the desiderata of various branches of knowledge, they would not be students; they would already have the competence which would make them eligible for election to the staff. I agree that there is everything to be said for teachers trying to discover, not only by observation but also by direct inquiry, what effect is produced by their teaching and whether the tradition of examination questions is thought to be fair. But we are on the other side of the limits of the desirable if students are given constitutional rights to have a hand in selecting teachers and administrators or to have a hand in the setting of standards. Eric Ashby somewhere relates the story of a deputation of students in an important part of the then Empire who on the occasion of the Diamond Jubilee of Queen Victoria approached the representative of the Crown to ask that in celebration of that august event, the standard of examination should be lowered for the next twelve months. I do not say that this would always be the tendency. But I am quite clear that academic constitutions should afford no loophole for any pressure of this sort.

There is a further and perhaps even deeper reason why the student body should not be admitted to powers involving control of the teaching process; it is fundamentally inimical to the main conception of academic freedom. If elections to chairs and the prescription of what shall and shall not be required for certification are to be within the power of the student body, there is critical danger. Again I do not for a moment say that such powers would *necessarily* be abused. But I do say that there is plenty of indirect evidence that their existence would introduce all sorts of irrelevant elements. And I cannot believe that conditions in which the appointment of teachers and the framing of courses were subject to student control, and perhaps student agitation, would be conducive to the free development of academic traditions, either by individuals or by institutions, which is so important if liberty of the intellect is to survive. The sort of student who agitates for student power is the sort of student who would readily lead a movement against a professional appointment which was disliked on political grounds. I am not in the least unaware of the dangers of academic freedom itself. It is a state of affairs which tends to be abused by unscrupulous academics and which, from time to time, may therefore mean that students suffer from mistaken appointments. But taking all this into account, I am sure that the admission of student control in this group of functions would bring with it less rather than more of the desirable aspects of academic freedom than we have at present.

Clearly, the extent to which I am disposed to make concessions to the overt movements for student power falls a good deal short of what the leaders of such movements would desire. But I must say at once, and with such emphasis as I can command, that this does not mean that I believe that the contemporary student has no real grievances. Indeed, I would argue that in any ultimate analysis, the grievances which I shall now discuss are considerably greater than any of the grievances which may arise from the lack of fulfillment of legitimate aspirations for more representation and more opportunities for participating in the machinery of academic government.

The first of these grievances arises because of the existence of large and inappropriately organized educational units. In my judgment the mere size of many universities today is such as to breed unrest and uneasiness in the student body. The individual on a campus of many thousands of undergraduates is apt to feel lost and bewildered—a sort of spiritual agoraphobia. He is an atom in a world of apparently unorganized atoms. There is no sense of community; and he and his fellow atoms are apt prey for any articulate neurotic who happens to come along and find his spiritual compensation in working on the emotions of others. It is no accident, I think, that many of the revolts of our time have taken place in universities which were either absolutely large in this sense, or were in a process of growth so rapid that the traditional forms of organization were proving inadequate.

But what is to be done about this? We ought not to denounce all bigness as such. I can believe that there are universities so large that they may merit this kind of condemnation on this ground alone. But the size of modern universities in general is not without its academic *raison d'être*. With the growth of knowledge and the consequent necessity for specialization among teachers and supervisors of research, up to a point at any rate, there are real advantages of scale in large organizations. However desirable it is to avoid premature specialization among students, we cannot just go back to a past with no large institutions with graduate schools beyond and no division of labor in the different spheres of research. I am sure that would not be conducive to an atmosphere appropriate to the needs of the twentieth century—either for staff or for students.

In my judgment, the solution is to be found in some sort of cellular organization—some organization which, while preserving for appropriate purposes the advantages of large-scale organizations, yet provides also units small enough to evoke human relations and human loyalties. If some such system is adopted, then the upper desirable limit on over-all size of the university need be much less restricted than where such systems do not prevail.

Of such forms of organization, I am inclined to think that the college system, or some variant thereof, is the best. I think it is no accident that at Oxford and Cambridge, where such systems prevail, although the total university populations are considerably greater than elsewhere in England (London, which is *sui generis,* excepted), there has been far less revolt among the students than in many smaller universities not so organized. If, for structural or constitutional reasons, a collegiate organization is impossible, then other expedients must be adopted. For the graduate school or advanced honors work, the department is an obvious basis to build upon, always provided that it is realized that something more than mere intellectual relations are involved. The real difficulty arises with general or joint course students not yet specialized in one direction; and it is here, of course, that the troubles of the student are likely to be greatest. I do not know any simple solution: I will only say that some sort of attachment to groups which give the student the sense of belonging—so important at all stages of life—seems to me quite imperative.

This brings me to the second real grievance of the contemporary student: the absence of effective contact with members of the staff. Let me be quite clear what I mean by this. I do not mean the absence of spoon-feeding. A great many

British students when ventilating their troubles are apt to demand what they call a "proper" tutorial system—by which they mean the system which used to prevail at our ancient universities whereby each student was entitled to one to two tutorial hours per week alone with a qualified teacher. But, with present numbers and present revenues, such a system is clearly out of the question for the majority of universities. It is indeed, in my judgment, intolerably wasteful at the undergraduate—as distinct from the graduate—level; and the fact that it is not generally adopted is no real grievance at all.

It is, however, a real grievance if there is no provision for contact, in less spendthrift ways, between students and teachers. It is a real grievance if from the moment of entering a university the student has no senior person to take an interest in his progress and to provide a personal link with the more permanent traditions of his institution. It is a real grievance if he is made to feel that he is regarded as a mere semimanufacture to be processed further through a vast learning machine, in order that funds may be procured to finance graduate studies and graduate research for which he himself may never qualify. Yet that, I am afraid, is the impression gained by many students in the larger universities of today.

What is the cause of this? To some extent it is defective organization. As institutions grow, the contacts which arise spontaneously when they are small tend insensibly to become more and more attenuated; and unless deliberate attempts are made to offset this tendency through the organization of classes and the personal discussion of written work, the atmosphere becomes more and more impersonal; and the student feels more and more just a unit in a purely mechanical universe.

But partly I believe it is due to certain influences on the attitude of teachers. Of course, all big institutions have their bad appointments: teachers who should never have been chosen, teachers who more or less deliberately neglect their duties. I am not thinking of such cases, difficult as they may be to deal with under some rules of tenure. I am thinking rather of the teacher who puts publication before teaching and who thereby gives his students the impression that he regards their presence as merely a necessary evil. This is not an imaginary case. With the growth of the habit of making publication the almost indispensable qualification for promotion, I should say it was becoming more and more general. Yet few habits could be more absurd. Some of the most valuable academic personalities of the past have published scarcely anything; certainly the inspiration of successive generations of students is at least as important, I should say, as nine-tenths of the contributions appearing in most of our learned journals. I say nothing in derogation of the advancement of learning—Heaven forbid. But publication is not the only way of creating the atmosphere in which this takes place. And so long as the manufacture of printed material weighing a minimum amount, so to speak, on the kitchen scales, is thought to be a better claim to a senior post than years of efficient and dedicated teaching, so long will be the gulf between university staffs and undergraduate students continue to increase.

Finally I come to the broader aspects of my assignment, the malaise generally apparent, not only among students, but among so many of the more lively and sensitive of the younger generation wherever they are. This is a wide and ambiguous subject not to be dealt with adequately in the concluding stages of an essay like this. I must therefore confine myself to a few crude generalities.

Let me say straightaway that by lively and intelligent youth, I do not mean the more vociferous and exhibitionist members of that generation. I am not thinking of the organized agitators, of whose activities in recent troubles only the most gullible must be ignorant. Nor am I thinking of the hippies, the provos, and all the other pseudo-farouche sects who figure so largely in discussions in the popular press of problems of this nature. In the United Kingdom, at least, no one who really knows the student world will regard these fringe revolutionaries and eccentrics as in any way representative of the majority of the youth of the present day, whom I certainly regard as being as serious and as fundamentally reasonable as any generation which has preceded them; and it is to them and their troubles that I wish to direct my attention.

Whether or not the attitude of this group has any parallel in earlier times, I do not doubt for a moment that it is one of

Present Discontents of the Student Age Group

disquiet and unease. In my opinion, the existence of this frame of mind is not open to question—you can only not believe in it if you never talk to anyone under twenty-five. The problem is to discover its origins.

It is sometimes said that this uneasiness of youth is due to the decline of belief in traditional religion. But I doubt very much if this is true. I do not wish to deny the importance in human history of this tendency, as regards both thought and manners. But I do not think it has much to do with the troubles of the contemporary young. The conceptions of the physical universe or of the descent and destiny of man which underlie Biblical literature, or indeed that of any of the historical world religions, ceased to be plausible quite a long time ago; and while this may have been slow to penetrate to the unreflecting, it cannot have been hid from many generations of intelligent youth long before the present age. Of course, it can be argued that if we all believed that everything that happens, however deplorable, is, in some mysterious way, the fulfillment of an omnipotent, omniscient, and benevolent will, many current perplexities and anxieties would be allayed—not only among the young. But this is not to say that these perplexities and anxieties are *positively caused* by the mere absence of such beliefs. That would be altogether too easy.

Much more important, I am sure, is the general erosion of belief in what may be called the liberal values. I do not think that the average member of advanced Western society actually behaves with less regard to the ultimate decencies than his predecessor fifty years ago: on the contrary, I fancy I detect an amelioration of manners which is in itself admirable. But belief in the institutional framework and social system which has fostered such changes has diminished. There is hardly any civic virtue or liberal institution which has not been subject to the acid of doubt; and the confusion of thought which has resulted has unquestionably bred a certain infirmity of purpose. Only the gutter ideologies are held with any great tenacity nowadays: Yeats's lines, "The best lack all conviction and the worst / Are filled with passionate intensity," may not be literally true, but they indicate an undeniable tendency.

Nevertheless, I do not hold this to be the main cause of the malaise. A period of confusion of thought is a challenge to bold spirits; I should not expect it to evoke the moods of frustration which are the more disquieting features of contemporary youthful psychology. To discover the causes of these we must look rather to the general insecurity of the future and the sense of almost complete impotence to do anything about it. Here, in my judgment, are to be found the ultimate roots of the current disquiet among the groups I am concerned with.

But is this so irrational? Are they not right in feeling that the prospects of the future are infinitely more precarious than ever before in history? No doubt many of us learn to live with the menaces hanging over us; it is necessary to be a little insensitive to maintain sanity in this respect. And so far as the young are concerned, I doubt if they are thinking about

Present Discontents of the Student Age Group

the ultimate possibilities every day. But the possibilities are there, and deep down they give an impermanence and an insecurity to the general outlook which colors the whole of these young people's lives. No doubt there has always been some tendency among the more emotional to see in contemporary dangers an ultimate threat to the future. The difference in this respect between today and former ages is that then it was possible to argue that most of these apprehensions were baseless—that after all civilized life was likely to persist—whereas today, if we are honest, we can give no such assurance. Has there ever been a period in the world's history which has witnessed a greater aggregate of injustice and horror than the last half century: the fratricidal slaughter of the nations of the West, the murderous tyrannies of the dictatorships of both the right and the left, the general collapse of international order? *Pendant que ça dure.* That surely is the secret assumption on which most of us of whatever age are tempted to act today. Can we really blame the less emotionally hardened if they are harrowed and distracted by the spectacle?

Are they to be blamed any the more if, faced with these potentialities and prospects, they are affected with a desolating sense of impotence and frustration? What assurance can we give them that those in control of events are in any sense equal to the occasion? Think calmly of the spectacle of a meeting of the United Nations—the organ which it was hoped would guard us from these dangers—with the dozens of splinter-state members frothing away in futile self-importance, all significant discussion blocked by a Byzantine procedure and a total absence of power to enforce anything. Think of the quality of the average oratory in the political assemblies of any democratic community—the empty clichés, the misleading generalities, the appeals to the gallery, the utter fourth-rateness of it all. We who have lived longer know, perhaps, how to ignore or to tolerate this—most of the orators are not such bad chaps after all. But who are we to condemn the more sensitive and candid who find it almost an ultimate betrayal of all to which they have been taught to attach value?

Thus, in the last analysis I find that the causes of distress among the young should cause distress to us all. Indeed, if we of the senior generation are not distressed and apprehensive, this is surely yet another vindication of the Shavian aphorism which I quoted at the beginning, that every man over forty is a scoundrel.

The Market versus the Bureaucrat

MILTON FRIEDMAN

THE topic for this symposium mirrors the widespread tendency to take it for granted that growth of population, advancing technology, expanding output of goods and services, increasing complexity of our industrial structure—the whole set of developments we label economic growth—necessarily repress individuality and enforce conformity. In the words of the brochure describing the symposium, "many thoughtful persons view these [scientific and technological] advances as creating new forms of bondage and as grave threats to the integrity of the individual."

I believe that this view is, to say the least, a great oversimplification. True, new forms of bondage are being created, and there are grave threats to the integrity of the individual. But the history of mankind—from primitive times to the present—is mostly a record of bondage, of tyranny of man over man. We do not need any sophisticated analysis to explain why freedom is threatened. Tyranny is the natural state of mankind. The remarkable thing about our era is the freedom we enjoy, not the threats to that freedom. And these threats themselves are not an inevitable consequence of the growing complexity of our society. They are a result of the social policies we have chosen to adopt. They are a result of a lack of understanding, not of harsh inevitability.

The causal relation between growth and freedom is almost the opposite of that which is commonly assumed: freedom produces growth and prosperity, and growth and prosperity in turn provide greater scope for freedom—though imperfect man may fail to grasp this potentiality and may instead use his material wealth to exploit his fellow man, in which case he will also destroy his prosperity.

Whether we look at the Golden Age of ancient Greece, or at the early centuries of the Roman era, or at the Renaissance, we see that widening individual freedom and quickening of economic growth went hand in hand—and that when freedom was destroyed, economic decline was not far behind. To come closer to our own times, the breaking down of feudal relations, the loosening of control over economic activity by the state, the widening of the scope assigned to individual initiative produced the great scientific and technological advances of the seventeenth and eighteenth centuries. It is no accident that the industrial revolution which followed had its home in Britain, where the ties of bondage were loosest, or that it had its greatest flowering after Britain adopted *laissez faire* as a national policy, or that the leadership moved to the United States at a time when we too had

The Market versus the Bureaucrat

limited intervention by the government into economic affairs.

These developments illustrate that great insight which Adam Smith expounded so effectively. The free market enables millions of men to cooperate with one another in complex tasks without compulsion and without centralized control. The invisible hand of the free market, whereby men who intend only to serve their own interests are led to serve the public interest, is a far more sensitive and effective source of both growth and freedom than the dead hand of the bureaucrat, however well intentioned he may be.

Growth and development do of course produce new problems of reconciling the freedom of one man with the freedom of others—problems of congestion, pollution, and so on. And many of these can best be met by coordinated action through governmental channels. But growth and development also reduce the problems of preserving freedom in other areas. For example, growth of population and improvements in transportation and communication have greatly widened the scope for effective competition and so have reduced the need for governmental concern with monopolistic behavior—though unfortunately, as most notably in transportation itself, we have often reacted by protecting entrenched monopoly from competition rather than taking full advantage of the new scope for competition.

Whatever may be the net balance of the effects of growth, the most obvious threats to the integrity of the individual have a very different source: in area after area of our national life, we have adopted policies that unnecessarily threaten the integrity of the individual. In each of these, there are alternative policies that would both promote our objective better and strengthen individual freedom. The areas in which this is true are varied, and they refer to many different aspects of our lives. Yet there runs through them a common element: the substitution of bureaucratic organization and control for market arrangements, the rejection of Adam Smith's great insight.

I shall illustrate this generalization by discussing three specific areas: radio and television, schooling, and public welfare. I have chosen three different areas out of the many available to show under how varied a guise the same basic issue arises.

Radio and Television

Here are marvelous technological achievements that we are failing to exploit effectively. We have a "wasteland" of highly repetitive, standardized programs directed at the great masses—which by itself is all to the good—but with all too little in the way of imaginative, exploratory, or simply high quality programs directed at minorities. The medium promotes deadening uniformity rather than variety, diversity, and individuality. The preferences of a minority, however strong they may be, must give way to the preferences of the mass audience, however weak.

Equally important, a medium that could promote vigorous and lively discussion of public issues seldom ventures into controversial areas. Truly free speech is held in check by the

The Market versus the Bureaucrat

fear of losing a license and is replaced by "fair" speech. The occasional slightly venturesome documentary or exposé is trumpeted far and wide as a sign of the independence of the station or network. The magnificent coverage of many news events—from the Olympics to the moon landing by American astronauts—shows the potential of the medium, so far largely unexploited.

This indictment is widely accepted. What has been the response? A string of privately supported educational television stations and, because these seemed inadequate, the enactment of a new Public Broadcasting Act under which the federal government will subsidize the production and distribution of programs. Talk about carrying coals to Newcastle. As we shall see, the problem is that there is now too much control by the federal government—through the Federal Communications Commission—over radio and television. To cure this, we establish another federal body to be a monopoly supplier of programs. To quote my colleague, Ronald Coase, who dubbed the measure "a wholly objectionable poverty program for the well-to-do," "the Public Broadcasting Act of 1967 is unnecessary, inefficient, inequitable and subject to dangerous political influences."

I suggest that the key to the present defect is the federal licensing of broadcasters. This gives the Federal Communications Commission the power of life and death over a station. If a person wants to start a newspaper, and has the capital, he needs merely buy a printing press, rent a location, publish his paper, and see if he can get the public to buy it. Once he is in business, his readers and advertisers are the only ones he must satisfy. But if he wants to set up a radio or television station, he also must convince the FCC that he is a person of good moral character and that there is a "need" for additional facilities. This may not be easy to do—ask those who have tried to get a license for Austin, Texas. And once the FCC grants him a license, he must satisfy it that he is presenting a "balanced" and "fair" program.

If newspapers were subject to the same controls, the *New York Times* would have to change its motto to "All the news that the FCC believes fit to print," and neither the *New York Times* nor the *Chicago Tribune,* as presently constituted, could conceivably get a clean bill of health. Fortunately, newspapers developed in an earlier era and have so far escaped control. Had they first developed in, say, the 1920s or 1930s, there would almost surely be today a Federal Publications Commission—as indeed was recommended in the famous Hutchins Report on the press.

One specific measure taken by the FCC has perhaps done more than any other single thing to stifle diversity and enshrine mediocrity. That is its refusal to authorize subscription or pay television. The FCC has ruled that we may not spend our money to see programs we wish to see. We must accept the programs that are provided as a by-product of advertising. We cannot even, if we wish to, pay to suppress the advertising, except by contributing to and watching an educational television station.

To understand how this measure has such a far-reaching

The Market versus the Bureaucrat

effect in enshrining mediocrity in television and radio, let us consider what the effect would be of applying the same rule in a comparable area to which it is not now applied. Suppose it were legislated that reading matter could not be sold but must be given away, that all newspapers must be like the "throwaways" now often given out, that all magazines must be available without charge, financed only by the revenue from the advertising they contain or by a subsidy from a church, foundation, or other organization, and similarly that any books published must be financed in the same way and distributed without charge to readers. It takes no great act of the imagination to see the results: those books and magazines that appeal to relatively small groups with specialized tastes would disappear. Few if any advertisers would deem it worthwhile to pay for the publication of avant-garde poetry in order to be able to insert pages extolling the virtue of Gleem or Dream or Steem. Far better to put those pages in a western that millions would pick up and read avidly. The book publishing industry would become like television—a wasteland of westerns, mysteries, and popular romances, with an occasional serious work appealing to a limited audience sponsored by a firm trying to improve its public image, or just with unusual tastes.

Your immediate reaction will be to regard this as a fantastic horror story and to dismiss it out of hand. But let me urge you not to let yourself be a victim of the tyranny of the status quo. The distribution of reading matter is almost strictly comparable to the distribution of television programs. I have not seen any argument in favor of forbidding pay television that does not apply with roughly equal force to forbidding pay publishing. And conversely—no argument in favor of pay publishing that does not apply with roughly equal force to permitting pay television. The two strike us as "of course" different only because they happen to have developed differently.

Why has the FCC prohibited pay television these past many years, except for a few so-called "pilot" projects? Because the networks are firmly established as the dominant distributors of national advertising, and they believe, rightly or wrongly, that they would fare less well than they do now if a new way of distributing programs were permitted. The networks exert enormous influence over the FCC—and it is inevitable that they should, just as it is inevitable that the railroads will exert enormous influence over the ICC, the banks over the Federal Reserve, and the producers of automobiles, over the federal agency to promote automobile safety. If the FCC had not stood in the way, pay television would now be a major factor, and the range, quality, and variety of television programs would now be far closer to that of book publishing.

How can we take advantage of the potentialities of television and radio and eliminate the present standardizing hand of the state? By abolishing the FCC and having a truly free radio and television to parallel a free press. But I will be told, that is absurd. There are only a limited number of television channels; someone must assign them. It is regrettable that we

The Market versus the Bureaucrat

should have to have federal control over radio and television, but that simply reflects the technological characteristics of the industry. Nothing of the sort. There are only a limited number of pieces of land on which a newspaper plant can stand. Why does that not require assignment of land? Because there is private property in land and the allocation of land can be performed by purchase and sale.

Precisely the same solution is available for radio and television. Let the FCC auction off to the highest bidders the rights to specified channels now embodied in licenses (for example, the right to broadcast on specified frequency from a specified location at specified times at a specified maximum power). That was what the federal government did a century and more ago with its land. The FCC could then be abolished. The private owners could trade these rights back and forth and rearrange them in various ways to make them more valuable. There would be problems of interference—of one man trespassing on another's frequency—but they would be handled as trespassing on land now is, through the regular courts.

I cannot here elaborate this proposal and consider all its implications in full detail, even if I had the competence to do so. Let me only state that this is not just a crackbrained, off-the-cuff suggestion. It is a proposal that has been extensively studied, in particular by R. H. Coase. All the serious objections raised have been examined. There is little doubt that it is a perfectly feasible way to handle the allocation and use of radio and television channels without special government control, little doubt that it would produce a far more efficient use of the radio spectrum, in many different ways, than prevails today. And, in terms of the theme of this conference, there is little doubt that it would convert what is today a homogenizing influence into a major force widening the avenues for the expression of individuality.

Schooling

For reasons of space, I shall restrict myself to higher schooling—or as it is euphemistically called, higher education. (Personally, I prefer the more descriptive term because not all schooling is education nor all education schooling.) I may, however, note that lower schooling offers an equally striking example of my main theme.

The trend is clear. Government expenditure on higher schooling has been growing rapidly. A steadily increasing fraction of students are enrolled in governmentally run institutions. There are more complaints about the impersonality of the mega-universities, the neglect of the individual student, the standardization and routinization of the educational process. And the private schools, like Reed, that provide a welcome contrast and that have been the leaders in fostering quality education, find it more and more difficult to compete for students and funds with the governmental institutions. They are themselves becoming increasingly dependent on tax monies for support.

These developments raise two separate issues: First, how much of a governmental subsidy, if any, there should be for

The Market versus the Bureaucrat

higher schooling; second, how any subsidy should be distributed.

Strictly speaking, only the second of these issues is relevant for my theme—how we have been unnecessarily curbing individuality by the social policies we have been following. But I cannot forbear from a few comments on the first issue, because I feel so strongly about it.[1]

The present use of tax monies to subsidize higher schooling seems to me one of the great suppressed scandals of our day. Compare the young men and women who receive this subsidy by attending state-supported institutions with their contemporaries who do not go to college at all. The youngsters in college come from higher income families than those who are not in college—but both sets of families pay taxes. More important, the youngsters in college will on the average have higher incomes for the rest of their lives than the youngsters who do not go to college. We have imposed a major tax on the poor to subsidize the not-so-poor. We in the middle- and upper-income classes have in this area—as I am afraid we have in many others—conned the poor into supporting us in a style that we take to be no more than our just deserts.

It is eminently desirable that every young man and woman, regardless of the wealth or religion or color or social standing of his or her family, have the opportunity to get whatever schooling he or she can qualify for, *provided that*

---

[1] These comments refer only to schooling, not to government expenditures for support of research, which raise a different set of issues.

79

he or she is willing to pay for it, either currently or out of the subsequent higher income that the schooling will make possible. There is, that is, a strong case for assuring the availability of loans or their equivalent, by governmental means, if necessary. There is no case that I can see for providing subsidies.[2]

Having relieved myself of these obiter dicta, let me turn to the second question: how should any subsidy be distributed? Currently, we distribute the subsidy primarily by having the government run institutions of higher learning and by charging tuition to students that is far below the costs incurred on their behalf. This is both inequitable and inefficient. Moreover, it is this practice, much more than the subsidization of higher schooling, that promotes conformity and threatens individuality.

Under current arrangements, the state of Oregon says to its young men and women, "If you meet certain academic standards, we shall automatically grant you a scholarship worth something like fifteen hundred or two thousand dollars a year regardless of 'need'—provided that you are smart enough to go to the University of Oregon or Oregon State. If you are so perverse as to want to go to Reed, let alone to Stanford or Harvard or Yale or the University of Chicago, not a penny for you." Surely, it would be more equitable to proceed instead along the lines of the G.I. educational benefits for veterans. Let whatever money the state of Oregon

---

[2] For a fuller discussion of this point see my contribution to a symposium in *The Public Interest,* No. 11 (Spring, 1968), pp. 108–12.

wants to spend on higher schooling be divided into the appropriate number of scholarships, each of, say, two thousand dollars per year, tenable for four years. Let there be a competitive exam—or some other method of selection—and let these scholarships be awarded to individuals to be used to attend any approved institutions of their choice that will in turn accept them. If Oregon wants to continue to run the University of Oregon, let that institution charge tuition sufficient to cover its costs, and compete on even terms with other institutions. If it is more attractive to students than other institutions, it will flourish; if not, it will decline.

Today, there is no reason for faculties and administrators of the existing state institutions to pay any attention to their students, except as this will indirectly affect the legislature which votes them funds. The thing for them to do, as they well know, is to engage in activities that will appeal to the legislature while paying to students the minimum attention that will keep them from being too obstreperous. This is the valid element in the drive for student power.

The arrangement I suggest gives the student a wider range of choice and enables him to exert more influence on the kind of schooling he is offered. It eliminates the present unfair competition between state-run and other institutions. It gives the faculties and administrations of state-run institutions an incentive to serve their students. It would open up the opportunity for new institutions to enter the field and seek to attract customers. The strengthening of competition would promote improvements in quality and foster diversity and experimentation. Because the money would go to individuals, not institutions, it would be clear who are the recipients of the subsidy and bring into the open this question of who should be subsidized. Also, it would give the individual greater freedom of choice, greater opportunity to express his own values and to develop his own capacities as effectively as possible.

All of these are advantages of the scholarship plan. But they are also, to speak cynically, the major political obstacles to its enactment. As usual in such matters, the people who would benefit from the change do not know that they would; the vested interests that have developed under the present arrangement will recognize the threat to them at once.

Public Welfare

The methods by which we subsidize the poor have the same defects as those by which we subsidize the rich: they involve giving too much power to bureaucrats to determine who gets the subsidy and in what form, too little power to the people who are being subsidized, and too little incentive to them to reduce the subsidy they receive.

The defects of our present welfare programs are by now widely recognized. In the midst of great prosperity, the welfare rolls mount. Once on the rolls, many people find it difficult to get off. We have been creating a permanent class of welfare recipients, who devote their energies to wheedling a bit more welfare for themselves or bringing pressure to bear to improve welfare payments rather than to raising their

The Market versus the Bureaucrat

own incomes to a level at which they can be off welfare. We have an army of welfare workers administering the system. They find themselves bogged down in paper work, engaged in being policemen and spies, with little time left to perform their proper function—helping the unfortunate people who are under their charge. The whole process is degrading for the welfare recipient and demeaning for the welfare workers.

What is wrong? At bottom, I conjecture, the belief that the state through administrative machinery can deal with persons needing assistance in the way one person spending his own money can deal with another person. If, out of charitable inclinations, a man takes an interest in someone suffering misfortune, it is entirely understandable that he may want to make a detailed investigation of that person's circumstances, to assure himself that the misfortune is real, that he will want to explore the items needed and provide help for those he thinks most urgent, and then try to guide the person he is assisting to use the help most effectively. But translate this into a large-scale governmental program, and it ends up as the kind of administrative nightmare we now have. The welfare workers are not distributing their own money, so there must be controls over them. The criteria of need must be standardized. The forms of help must be specified. The dispersers of funds must be supervised. In the process, the human element is squeezed out and replaced by frustration and mutual distrust.

This system clearly is a "grave threat to the integrity of the individual" receiving welfare. Before a welfare recipient may move from one apartment to another, he must get the approval of a civil servant; equally, before he may buy secondhand furniture, have the gas turned on, or make any one of a thousand other deviations from an approved budget. Needless to say, the welfare recipients have become skilled in finding ways around the regulations, but nonetheless, the whole atmosphere is one in which they are treated like irresponsible wards of the state, like children, not like responsible citizens. Clearly, if the taxpayer does subsidize them, he has in some sense the moral right to impose such requirements. But is it wise to do so?

Most important of all, carrying over the notion of meeting the other person's "needs" has had the unfortunate effect of largely eliminating any incentive for the welfare recipient to help himself. If a welfare recipient earns an extra one hundred dollars, that is interpreted as meaning that he or she can meet an additional one hundred dollars of "needs," and therefore that welfare aid can be reduced by one hundred dollars. In consequence, the recipient has no incentive to earn money unless he can earn enough completely to replace welfare. This is the main reason why there tends to develop a permanent class of welfare recipients.

As in each of the two prior examples, the way to improve the situation is to put greater reliance on impersonal market arrangements and less on bureaucratic administration. For welfare, the device that recommends itself is the negative income tax, under which all persons with incomes below the level now taxable would be entitled to receive a fraction of

The Market versus the Bureaucrat

their unused exemptions and deductions. This method would give assistance to the poor in the form of money, which they could spend as they wish, on the basis of the impersonal criteria of the size of their income and the number of persons in their family, and in such a way as to give them an incentive to raise their income from other sources.

This is not the place for a detailed exposition of the way a negative income tax would work or of its advantages and disadvantages. It is sufficient for the present purpose to note that it has been studied carefully and that there is every reason to believe that it would be a feasible substitute for the present direct relief and aid to dependent children programs; that it would, over a period, simultaneously give more assistance to the truly needy and cost the taxpayer less.

The crucial point for our present purpose is that a negative income tax would permit the elimination of the bulk of our present welfare bureaucracy, would end the division of our population into two classes, would give those receiving assistance greater freedom and independence to shape their own life and greater opportunity to take advantage of their own abilities and capacities. In addition, whereas our present programs have essentially destroyed private philanthropy, the negative income tax, by assuming the basic load of income maintenance, would reduce the hardship cases, which no general program can eliminate, to a level that private charity could handle. We have been stifling private philanthropic agencies, converting them to agents or contractors of the state, by our conception of government welfare. The negative income tax would give them a new function to perform. The diversity, flexibility, and efficiency of free enterprise has a role to play in philanthropy no less than in other areas.

Conclusion

In recent decades, there has been a steady tendency to enlarge the role of the government, either to undertake new tasks or to take over tasks formerly entrusted to private and voluntary action. By now the process has gone very far indeed, even in a country like the United States which prides itself on being the country of free enterprise. Today, probably over one-third of all the income of the people in this country is channeled through the government—being extracted by taxes and loans, and spent for governmental programs. And this grossly understates the influence of the government. The wages many an employer may pay, the prices many an industry may charge, the businesses we may enter, the countries to which we may travel, and many other aspects of our daily lives are subject to governmental control.

This expansion of the role of the government has been sold to the American people on the ground that it would enhance both their material well-being and their personal freedom. And further expansion is now being sold to them on the same ground. The promises have been and remain glowing. Yet, when we look at performance and not promise, the story is very different. We have adopted reform after reform, program after program, without achieving the promised objectives. Consider those programs which have one

The Market versus the Bureaucrat

after the other been proclaimed as great progressive achievements: the National Recovery Administration, the Agricultural Adjustment Act and its successors; the Securities and Exchange Commission; public housing; the Wagner Labor Act; social security; relief and aid to dependent children; urban renewal; federal aid to education—which of them has achieved the objectives that aroused such high hopes in their disinterested supporters? The problems each was touted as solving are with us yet, often in exaggerated form. Or pass from the dramatic federal level to the local level. What are the major governmental responsibilities at the local level? Schooling and police protection. What are major areas of social concern? Inadequate schooling and crime on the streets.

It is a fascinating question of political science to explain this sequence of events. What is it that explains what activities are taken over by government and when? Why is it that so many measures work in accordance with the original intentions of the disinterested for a year or two, but then soon become devices whereby special interests enrich themselves? Why is it, that is, that well-intentioned liberals have so often turned out to be front men for special interests they would never knowingly have supported? Why is it that, in a democracy supposedly run by a majority, there are so many measures pandering to special interests?

These questions take us far afield from the more limited object of this paper: to show by example that the lack of success of many government programs and the threats they raise to freedom and individuality is a necessary consequence of neither the objectives sought nor the increasing complexity of our society. Television and radio, higher schooling, and welfare arrangements are very different areas in which we have very different objectives. Yet there is a common strand running through all three. In all, we have tried to substitute central direction and bureaucratic control for voluntary arrangements. In all, we could achieve our objectives far better by using arrangements that give a greater scope to the market, that rely on "participatory democracy" rather than on bureaucratic democracy.

If we are to meet the recurrent threats to freedom that are bound to arise, it is important that the informed public become more sophisticated than it is now about government programs. It must come to understand that the business community has no monopoly on misleading advertising, that promises must be distinguished from performance. We must try to repress the tendency to say, "Let's pass a law," whenever a problem arises and recognize that the indirect route through voluntary action may be surer and safer than the direct route through government action. And when we do turn to government action, we shall do best if, so far as possible, we try to restrict government action either to setting up arrangements under which private action can be effective (as in radio or television), or to giving money in an open and aboveboard way to specific individuals under specified conditions rather than to providing the relevant good or service by a government organization.

Prejudice and Politics in the American Past and Present*

SEYMOUR MARTIN LIPSET

THE social tensions inherent in rapid economic growth, urbanization, immigration, migration, and shifts in the position of different ethnic groups, have repeatedly stimulated in American history the phenomenon of the political "backlash." Various groups have experienced such changes as challenges to their status, values, or interests, and have reacted by seeking to eliminate the source of these threats which they have often located in the supposed control over the government, or the institutions which dominate communications and culture, by an immoral, corrupt, and un-American minority whose covert power has made the formal democratic process meaningless. Extremist movements—such as the Anti-Masonic party of the late 1820s, the various nativist

---

* This essay has also been published in Charles Y. Glock and Ellen Siegelman (eds.), *Prejudice: U.S.A.* (New York: Praeger, 1969). It is derived from a larger work, S. M. Lipset and Earl Raab, *The Politics of Unreason: Right-Wing Extremism in the United States, 1790–1970* (New York: Harper and Row, 1970).

and Know-Nothing anti-Catholic parties and orders of the pre-Civil War era, the American Protective Association of the 1890s, the Ku Klux Klan of the 1920s, the Coughlinite movement of the 1930s, the McCarthyite syndrome of the 1950s, and most recently the George Wallace movement in the 1960s—have each in different ways given expression to the sense of frustration that millions of Americans feel toward a threat to their power and status, or economic position.

The use of prejudicial ethnic, racial, and religious appeals against the supposed threat of minority groups is almost as old as the American political system itself. The efforts of nearly every minority group in the United States to improve its situation have been viewed as a threat by some who possessed dominant status-characteristics, and some political leaders at almost every period have appealed to such resentments to get votes.

How do these extremist appeals become crystallized in a political movement or a political party? Working on the model proposed by Neil Smelser, we can postulate the following: There must be first a social strain or decline in status which is somewhat ambiguous and creates widespread anxiety. The adherents of extremist movements have typically felt deprived—either they have never gained their due share, or they are losing their share, of power and status. We might call these two groups the "never-hads" and the "once-hads." These deprived groups are not necessarily extremist, but extremism usually draws its strength from them. The first type (never-hads) primarily tends to experience economic deprivation and consequently to seek redress by state action to achieve economic reforms; this experience typically has supported left-wing extremism, although it has occasionally fostered right-wing movements as well. The second type (once-hads) experiences or fears loss of status and influence; this group cannot be assuaged by government action. It requires a different course of action—usually the projection of grievances on to a minority group and attempts to discredit or destroy that group to relieve its own sense of anxiety. This typically takes the form of right-wing extremism, and it is with such extremism that we will be concerned with our focus on prejudice.

Such reactions are not simply a response to political changes and demands. The fluidity of the American social structure, the fact that no dominant group has ever enjoyed a socially recognized claim to long-term status in the style of some of the more status-bound class-ridden societies of the Old World, has meant that the problem of status insecurity has been an enduring characteristic of American life. New regions, new industries, new migrant groups, new ethnic and religious groups have continually encroached upon the old. These changes have often been accompanied by adjustments in the prevailing norms concerning proper relations between parents and children, the drinking of alcoholic beverages, the use of drugs, the relations between the sexes, styles of dress, conceptions of religious morality, and the like. Such changes in morality lead those adhering to the old norms to feel disinherited, dispossessed, displaced in their own land.

Groups who have a claim to status and cultural influence as a result of past or present achievements turn against existing political institutions when they feel that their claim is insecure, is under attack, or is actually declining. Under present conditions such groups may include some among the quite privileged, such as doctors or heads of family-owned corporations who feel the weight of growing government controls—or on a less affluent level, working-class whites who after gaining economic security feel the pressure of Negro demands on their schools, neighborhoods, and unions —or on an ideological axis, those whose self-identity is closely linked to traditional religious and secular values which appear to be in the process of being supplanted by concepts and behavior which they view as immoral. These are the prototypical situations which have fed the wellsprings of right-wing movements and, indeed, of right-wing extremism.

How do these groups whose status and values are threatened react to such insecurity? As Smelser suggests, they deal with it by designating a specific cause for that strain—not necessarily or typically the real cause, but a plausible one. In many cases, ethnically or religiously identifiable population groups have served that purpose well. The heavy immigration by ethnic groups who have allegedly introduced "un-Protestant" and "un-American" values and modes of behavior into this society has often been identified by "displaced" strata as the main threat to their values or position. So, for example, economic unrest has engendered mass anti-immigrant and anti-Catholic movements among the less privileged classes based on the charges that "alien" competition for jobs was the cause of unemployment. And loss of elections, the growth of urban machine politics, and changes in the general state of social morality commonly have been interpreted by groups losing their economic, social, political, or religious dominance as the fault of foreign and non-Protestant groups who have undermined the traditional structure of status and authority. Because nativism has so openly traded on religious and ethnic group appeals, it has been of primary importance in determining the correlations between party choice and membership in specific religious and ethnic groups. In most instances in this country the values that the declining majority has tried to preserve against the rising minorities have been the values of nativism, fundamentalism, and simplistic moralism.

Such moralism—operating as it does largely among the less educated, more fundamentalist, and more provincial—requires that the minority target group is held to be conspiring to destroy the very values that the deprived group is seeking to preserve. Conspiracy theories uniformly describe a high-powered core of intellectuals involved in devious manipulation of the national mind. As we shall see, conspiracy theories have provided the central drive for bigoted American political movements, because they suggest the course of direct action the deprived group must take: the remedy against the alleged conspiratorial plotting of a secret band of intellectuals at the helm of a distrusted minority group is exposure, repression, and even annihilation. And this course of action is presumably justified by the tenets of morality. The moralism of bigotry tends to be absolutist—the "enemy" is identified with the circulation of corrupt literature and with general debauchery. This black-and-white view insists that the enemy is debarred by its moral corruption and conspiratorial tactics from having any legitimate place in the normal political marketplace. This entire process can be called backlash politics, and it has characterized segments of American conservatism for much of our country's history.

The first such example involved New England Federalists, Congregationalists, and merchants, who reacted to their decline by discovering foreign-based conspiracies, and by emphasizing religion and moralism. In the last years of the eighteenth century they placed the blame for the changing moral order, and their concomitant loss of political power, religious influence, and status, on the conspiratorial activities of the Illuminati, an Enlightenment Society of intellectuals affiliated to the Masons, which existed for a brief period in Bavaria. Some European writers credited the group with responsibility for the French Revolution and other upheavals in various countries. The anti-Illuminati agitation involved an effort to defeat the rapidly growing Jeffersonian and deist challenges to the position and values of the Congregationalist and Federalist elites by identifying these opponents as agents of a revolutionary conspiracy.

A quarter of a century later, a new wave of exposés of Masonic, and to some extent Illuminati, conspiracies arose during a comparable period in which conservative political and traditional religious forces felt themselves under attack from the rising Jacksonian democracy and irreligious elements. The politically potent anti-Masonic movement drew much of its extensive support from the less educated, poor segments of the rural population which lived away from urban settlements, but it ultimately joined forces with the conservative National Republicans to form the Whig party. Both waves of agitation against Illuminati-Masonic conspiracies also involved links to ethnic and religious bigotry. The Illuminati of 1798 were identified with the revolutionary activities of the Irish in Ireland and America, while the Anti-Masonic party at times espoused nativist, anti-Catholic, and even anti-Semitic sentiments.

Such efforts to identify threats to the religious order and status system with hidden conspiracies, as well as the repeated espousal of anti-Catholic nativism, first by the Federalists and later by the Whigs and related groups, in the two decades before the Civil War, illustrate, as we shall see, the willingness of segments of the American elite to encourage extremism in their attempts to hold power. Among the masses, the rise of such movements has frequently represented the responses of evangelical Protestants to the changes that they feared were eroding their moral values or social status.

From the early days of the Republic down to the Great Depression, the most important source of prejudice in American politics was anti-Catholicism. Such sentiments have deep religious roots in this country: the Puritans and the Protestant sects, the Methodists and Baptists, who came to dominate in terms of numbers, all hated the Papists. And this deep streak of anti-Catholic feeling was seized on at different times in American history to sustain movements which sought to preserve existing institutions against the threat of change—a threat that was attributed to the increased number of Catholics in the country and even to conspiracies directed by Rome.

Perhaps the earliest sustained anti-Catholic political effort occurred in New York in the first decade of the nineteenth century. The recently defeated Federalist party, in an effort to regain strength by appealing to voters' religious prejudice, re-formed as the anti-Catholic American party,[1] thus initiating the oft-repeated pattern of conservatives resorting to appeals to racial or religious bigotry when they find their power declining.

Anti-Catholicism made its first independent political impact during the 1830s, coinciding with the increase of immigration and with the rise of Jacksonian Democracy. During this time a growing anti-Catholic literature reported the alleged sins and evil designs of the church, including revelations of secret sexual activities which presumably went on in convents and monasteries (*Six Months in a Convent, The Nun*, and others). The Catholics were described as seeking to conquer and corrupt America through sheer numbers—the inpouring of masses of Irish and other immigrants. Scattered

---

[1] This group was the first to introduce the name "American party." Some version of the term "American party" has been used by racists and bigots for well over a century and a half.

anti-Catholic parties appeared in eastern cities in the 1830s and grew in numbers and influence in the 1840s.

To a considerable degree the success of this wave of anti-Catholic hysteria seems to be linked to the weakness in the cities during the 1830s and 1840s of the principal conservative party, the Whigs. With the mass base given to the Democrats by the Jacksonian populist image, the Whigs found it increasingly difficult to win elections. They began to blame their defeats at the polls on the fact that foreigners and Catholics were voting overwhelmingly for the Democrats. As more and more foreigners, particularly Catholics, came into the country, many Whigs feared that they would be unable to compete effectively with their political rivals. This fear forced them on a number of occasions from the early 1840s on to compromise with their presumed dislike of appealing to prejudice by allying themselves with the more aggressively anti-Papist forces organized in the various small parties extolling an America-for-Americans nativism.

The use of anti-Catholicism by the Whigs played on a number of basic Protestant fears and values in an attempt to wean Protestants away from the Democrats. Orthodox Protestants saw in the growing number of Catholics and their increased political influence in the cities a threat to Protestant cultural dominance. The growing number of immigrants—Catholics and others—was regarded as a competitive economic and status threat by many Protestant workers. Furthermore, during this period of rapid population growth and geographic mobility, many Protestants moved from rural to urban areas, and in doing so severed their close social ties to the people and the institutions among which they were reared; they naturally feared the new ways of the city. The Protestants also feared the outcome of Catholic attempts to oppose Protestant teaching and the reading of the Protestant Bible in the public schools (the Catholics were supported in this demand by religious liberals, deists, and atheists, mainly united in the Democratic party).

Exploiting all these fears of economic, cultural, and moral displacement, the elaborately ritualistic anti-Catholic secret orders were able to recruit large numbers of Protestants, especially the poor and uneducated, to defend the old values and traditions. The literature that emerged in this period was not only anti-Catholic in general, but actually articulated a specific theory of Catholic conspiracy stemming from Rome, supposedly launched to undermine the American system. Belief in this theory presumably justified violent and undemocratic means to eradicate the conspiracy. From the 1840s to the mid-1850s violent anti-Catholic riots occurred. Churches and convents were burned and Catholics were beaten. Meanwhile, the Catholics were blamed for urban crime and the growth in immorality.

Given the rationale of moral absolutism, many of the same invidious things that are written openly or said privately about Negroes today were stated about other visible minority groups (primarily Catholic immigrants) at various periods before the Civil War. The themes of crime in the streets, immorality and unfitness, and conspiracy have been staples in the American diet of intolerance.

This rising tide of anti-Catholicism culminated in the emergence of the American, or Know-Nothing, party in 1854. The latter became for a brief period the second largest party in the United States, since the Whigs generally ceased to run candidates. It captured the government in many eastern cities, as well as Baltimore and New Orleans. Its representatives constituted two-thirds of the Massachusetts Legislature and a majority in the Connecticut Legislature. In fact, the Know-Nothing party had political hegemony in most of New England and in many of the Middle Atlantic states.

The political conditions which fostered the rapid growth of the Know-Nothing party closely resembled those linked to the spread of the anti-Illuminati agitation in the late 1790s and of the Anti-Masonic party at the end of the 1820s. The rise to prominence of the anti-conspiratorial movements seems to have been a reaction to the breakdown of the principal conservative political forces of each period. The anti-Illuminati frenzy coincided with the decline of federalism under John Adams, the Anti-Masons arose with the defeat of his equally conservative son John Quincy Adams and the rise of Jacksonian democracy, and the emergence of the Know-Nothings as a mass movement occurred after the breakup of the Whig party following its defeat in the election of 1852.

Although most American party votes clearly came from

former Whig supporters, the new party was able to win in traditional Democratic areas, particularly in cities, by capturing the backing of many Protestant workers who had previously voted Democratic. In some communities, it even took on a left or populist aura on various social issues.

But the Know-Nothings had a relatively short political career. The party broke up by 1857 before it could do much about Catholics or immigrants. It was torn asunder by the slavery issue, which was far more crucial for many devout Protestants than was the anti-Catholic cause. The northern supporters of the Know-Nothings were devoutly anti-slavery, and the southern supporters were equally committed to slavery. A moralistic based party so divided on so crucial an issue could not easily maintain itself.

In the North the Know-Nothings were absorbed into the new party which expressed the feeling of the middle-class, Protestant, formerly Whig community—the Republicans. The Republican party after the Civil War was to take over the role of the Know-Nothings as the anti-Catholic party. Ulysses S. Grant had been a Know-Nothing for a brief period. As commander of the Union Army during the Civil War, Grant had tried to bar Jews from areas he controlled. As a Republican President, he made overtly anti-Catholic public statements. In addressing a reunion of Union veterans, he spoke out about the threat of a new civil war between the supporters of superstition (that is, the Catholics) and the true believers; he intimated that the Union Army might have to be recalled to defend the country against the conspiracies of the forces of superstition. Both of Grant's vice presidents had been Know-Nothing leaders before the Civil War. Other Republican presidents and candidates, like Rutherford Hayes and James G. Blaine, were also active in the anti-Catholic fight. On the local level, in the cities the role of the Republicans as an anti-Catholic party was even more obvious. The statement which supposedly defeated Blaine in the presidential election of 1884 was the Reverend O. O. Blanchard's accusation that the Democrats were "the party of rum, Romanism, and rebellion." Many historians have been so unaware of the role of religion as a perennial source of post-Civil War partisan controversy that for a long time this one slogan was mentioned as having had a decisive effect on the election's outcome. Yet this single allegation could hardly have defeated Blaine, for thousands of Republicans had said the same or worse. Blanchard could legitimately be regarded as having merely epitomized what many Republicans were saying all along.

Two efforts to recreate a party called the American party during this period failed. The first, which ran presidential candidates in 1876 and 1880, represented a minor effort by provincial Protestant fundamentalists to revive an anti-Masonic movement, with tinges of anti-Catholicism. Some of the literature of this movement linked radical activities of the day, such as the Paris Commune of 1871 and the American strike wave of the seventies, with the continued activities of the Illuminati, previously credited with having organized the French revolutions of 1789 and 1830. The second American party of the post-Civil War era was formed in the late 1880s and was primarily anti-Catholic and nativist. Although it tried to mount a national campaign, it, too, found little support for a third party.

Although efforts to form a new party based on Protestant conspiracy fears failed, conditions had changed sufficiently by the end of the eighties to facilitate the growth of a militantly anti-Catholic movement, the American Protective Association (APA), which was founded in 1887.

At its high point in 1893, the APA and its allied organizations were credited with a membership of about two million people. In approach, the APA echoed the Know-Nothings. It repeated many of the Know-Nothing tales of Catholic conspiracy, warned Americans that the Catholics were arming to seize power and kill off Protestants, and accused the Catholics of having assassinated Presidents Lincoln and Garfield. So intense was the anti-Catholic feeling, and so widely held was the conspiracy theory, that a responsible public official, the governor of Ohio, in 1893 issued arms to Protestants to defend themselves against the alleged Catholic plan to kill them. The APA at the time was buying rifles and drilling troops because of its belief that on a specific day the Catholics were going to shoot the Protestants in a manner reminiscent of the St. Bartholomew's Day Massacre in sixteenth-century France. Hundreds of thousands—perhaps millions—of Protestants took this allegation so seriously that they felt they must bear arms to defend themselves against the threat from the Catholic minority. The proportion of Catholics was then not more than that of Negroes now—about 15 per cent; the phenomenon of the 85 per cent of the population fearing that they were going to be shot down in their beds and wiped out by the 15 offers eerie parallels with the contemporary situation.

This dramatic rise of the APA in the early 1890s, like that of the Know-Nothings in the 1850s, seems to have been related to a visible threat to the political domination of the major source of evangelical Protestant control—in this case, the Republican party. In the congressional elections of 1890, the Republican party suffered its greatest defeat since its formation, shifting from a House majority to a minority of 88 members, as compared to 235 Democrats and 9 Populists. In 1892, the Democrats won the presidency with their first decisive plurality since 1856. They also held political control of many cities, in which Irish Catholics were beginning to take over as mayors and political leaders. Issues concerning teaching in the public schools continued to divide Protestants and Catholics. Many descendants of the first group of Catholic and Jewish immigrants who had come in before the Civil War now were prosperous second- and third-generation Americans, demanding the right of access to high-status institutions. Other pressures during the 1890s came from increasing immigration from Europe and rapid industrialization and urbanization. In addition, the depression of 1893, leading to more competition for scarce jobs, further stimulated the growth of the APA among the fearful Protestant workingmen, who constituted a large segment of the APA membership at its height. The APA for the most part worked in and through the Republican party (although in some areas it also received support from Populist leaders), much as some previous anti-Catholic, nativist movements had worked in and through the Whig party.

The APA, like the Know-Nothings, flourished for only three or four years, declining in large part because the Republican leadership, many of whom had encouraged it while the Democrats were in power, turned against it after their overwhelming victories in the depression-influenced 1894 congressional elections. This success, for which the APA tried to claim credit, suggested to party leaders like Mark Hanna that they had an opportunity to win over the urban Catholic and immigrant vote if they disassociated themselves from bigoted groups like the APA.

The repudiation of the APA by leading Republicans, some of whom like William McKinley had earlier encouraged it, illustrates an oft-recurring pattern in the political life of the United States. The moderate conservatives (Whigs or Republicans) when at a low political ebb occasionally encouraged racism or political extremism—overtly or covertly—as a way of winning over some of the less privileged among their Democratic opponents. Such alliances were usually short-lived, since the moderates typically turned on the extremists as a result either of electoral success or of the growing revulsion against the increasingly overt bigotry of the extremists.

While anti-Catholicism was the main source of religious bigotry in the nineteenth century, anti-Semitism, which was to become so important in the twentieth century, was also beginning to send up visible shoots. Growing out of the soil of rural America, particularly in the West, anti-Semitism first appeared in political literature in the United States in the 1870s as part of the agrarian response to the depression of 1873. Agrarian protest organizations blamed the decline of farm prices and the other economic difficulties of farmers on the banks which manipulated the value of money, held farm mortgages, and charged high interest in the New York and international exchanges. In the late nineteenth century the international figures who controlled these banks were often personified as Jews, and financiers like the Rothschilds were treated as symbols of evil. The literature of the agrarian-based Populist party of the 1890s sometimes talked darkly of international financial conspiracies designed to destroy America; some of the Populist leaders were overt anti-Semites as well as active APA members.

The APA, like the Know-Nothings, had considerable strength in urban areas among workers, including trade unionists, particularly in western states. Eugene Victor Debs, then a railroad union leader, found it necessary to wage a campaign against the divisive influence of the APA within union ranks. Populism had considerable support among provincial evangelical Protestants in the rural areas of midwestern and southern America. And in some communities, though linked to the APA, populism constituted an alternative rural form of protest against the urban, cosmopolitan, eastern elites. Though strands of anti-Catholicism and anti-Semitism were present within it, on the whole the Populists defined the source of conspiracy which threatened their livelihood and social system in economic class terms, that is, in the activities of bankers and businessmen. In a sense, both the APA and the Populists gave expression to a tendency of provincial Americans, located away from the economically and culturally dominant cities of the East, to regard these centers as dens of iniquity and economic exploitation. The process of pitting the provincial Americans—heavily small-town rural Protestant—against the secularized wealthy urban elites, has been a continuous one in the political life of this country. As part of this process, after the turn of the century some former Populists shifted their target from urban elites generally to the city-dwelling Catholics and Jews specifically.

The most prominent exponent of this new theme of bigotry was Tom Watson, who had been the major Populist party leader in the South. Watson had opposed the merger of the Populists with the Democrats in 1896. In various newspapers he continued the Populist diatribes against bankers, capitalists, and railroad magnates, but also increasingly expounded a violent form of racial and religious bigotry directed at Catholics, Jews, and Negroes. Watson's paper, *The Jeffersonian,* published in a small town in Georgia and circulated widely throughout the country, broadcast his contention that Jews and Catholics were united in a conspiracy to take over America. Watson became best known before the United States entered World War I for his leadership in the effort to convict and later lynch an Atlanta Jew, Leo Franks, for the murder of a young girl. Watson seized on this case, and particularly on the efforts of Jews and liberals to defend Franks, as proof of the conspiracy of wealthy Jews to use and mistreat poor Christians.

Following World War I and during the prosperous decade of the 1920s, the United States experienced its most drastic period of repression, typified by the rise of the anti-Catholic, anti-Negro, anti-Semitic, and anti-intellectual Ku Klux Klan. The Klan was founded in 1915 by the members of an organization originally set up by Watson to help convict Leo Franks. With an estimated membership in the 1920s of three to six million, the Klan drew its members not only from the South but from many northern states, and elected governors, mayors, and legislators all over the country. It received considerable support in the burgeoning cities both in and out of the South—cities growing by virtue of the large number of recent small-town migrants. These migrants sought to preserve the rural values of their upbringing and saw in the Klan a means to assure "law and order" in their new urban environment.

The Klan charged that Catholics and Jews had allied to dominate the cultural and economic life of the country and that in conjunction with the Communists they were seeking to take over the government by force.[2] The Klan also revived the charges that Catholics had been involved in the killings of Presidents Lincoln, Garfield, and McKinley. It even argued that President Warren G. Harding was murdered in 1923 by a secret, undetectable Catholic weapon—presumably evidenced by the fact that his death certificate read "cause unknown" and no autopsy was performed (it was generally agreed that Harding actually died of a coronary embolism). Anti-Semitism was also a leading Klan leitmotif. One Klan leader held that Jewish international bankers were responsible for starting World War I; others charged that the Jews had organized the Bolshevik Revolution and were behind communism everywhere. Some Klan leaders combined the Catholic and Jewish conspiratorial themes, suggesting that Jews and Catholics were united in a plan to control the nation's press, economy, and political life. They pointed to New York as an example of a depraved city controlled by Jews and Catholics.

Given the concern with changing values, new "freer" ideas, and the loss of religious values, it is not surprising that the Klan leaders also attacked intellectuals, whom they identified with the growth of "liberalism." They were described by a Klan leader as "one of the chief menaces of the country, instead of the sane intellectual leaders they should be. They

[2] At this period Negroes were not felt to be as much of a threat as Catholics or Jews; although the Klan was strongly against Negro equality, its attacks of the early twenties did not fall on Negroes as heavily as on Catholics or Jews.

give an almost joyous welcome to alien criticism of everything American."

Although the Klan attacked immigrants and Negroes, who were economically deprived, it did not see itself as a conservative defender of white Protestant privileges. Rather, according to Emerson Loucks, the most successful Klan spokesmen found that the best way to appeal to prospective followers was by casting "the native white Protestant not as belonging to the predominant and controlling group . . . but as the oppressed poor, oppressed sufferer, plundered by foreigners, tricked by 'Jesuits' and robbed of his birthright by scheming descendants of Abraham." Ironically, they, too, appealed to "the sympathy generally shown by the mass of Americans to the underdog, the fellow they feel hasn't had a fair chance." Thus the Klan, like its predecessors from the Anti-Masons on, linked itself to the anti-elitist and equalitarian tradition of the country, while spreading bigotry.

The twenties also saw the emergence of Henry Ford as a respected spokesman for right-wing extremism and religious prejudice. Through his violently anti-Semitic newspaper, the *Dearborn Independent,* Ford reached more than seven hundred thousand readers. For years the *Dearborn Independent* hammered away at the theme of an international Jewish conspiracy. A series of eighty articles in the paper were reprinted in book form as *The International Jew: The World's Foremost Problem.* More than half a million copies of this extremely anti-Semitic book were distributed throughout the United States. The articles in it bore such titles as

"Jewish Gamblers Corrupt American Baseball," "How the Jewish Song Trust Makes You Sing," "Jew Wires Direct Tammany's Gentile Puppets," "The Scope of Jewish Dictatorship in America," "The Jewish Associates of Benedict Arnold." In short, Ford blamed the Jews for everything from communism to jazz, immorality, and short skirts.

Ford would not be of much interest to the story of political prejudice had he not been boomed as a possible presidential candidate in 1923. Then at the height of his well-publicized campaign of anti-Semitism, he was widely supported across the country. In fact, one of the early opinion polls reported that 35 per cent of its respondents preferred Ford for president.

Henry Ford's activities dramatized the entry into the American political arena of full-scale anti-Semitism. The Jews were eminently vulnerable to the new turn in conspiracy theory: they were visible in both radical and capitalist circles, although their numbers were wildly exaggerated. They were also castigated in the contemporary conspiracy theories that had been spawned for political purposes in Germany and in Tsarist Russia.

It is interesting to note the continuity in the conspiracy literature of the right. The Ku Klux Klan reprinted and circulated many books and stories about Catholic activities which had originated with the Know-Nothings or their predecessors. Ford and the Klan repeated reports about the efforts of Jewish international bankers to control and undermine the American financial system, which first emerged among the agrarian and Populist movements of the 1870s and 1890s. Most interesting of all was the renewed references to the conspiracy of the Illuminati. The staid *Christian Science Monitor* published an editorial in 1920, "A Jewish Peril?" which seriously discussed for a column and a half whether the Elders of Zion or the Illuminati were behind various revolutionary events and political turmoil from Russia to America. The *Dearborn Independent* reminded its readers that on two occasions in early American history, men had become aware that the country was threatened by hidden conspiratorial forces, that is, in 1798, when the Illuminati had first been attacked, and in the late 1820s during the campaign against the Masons. Ford's paper, however, argued that these earlier campaigns had failed because they had not realized that the true conspirators were the Jews, that the Illuminati were only a front for the Elders of Zion.

The 1920s not only had its extremist movements, such as the Klan, and its extremist political figures, such as Henry Ford; it also wrote its racial, ethnic, and religious bigotry and its moral absolutism into law. Thus, the period between the end of World War I and the mid-1920s saw the enactment of the following: restrictive immigration legislation—legislation that not only limited the total number of immigrants drastically but also set national quotas which discriminated against people of non-northern European, non-Protestant background, that is, Catholics and Jews; the prohibition amendment outlawing alcoholic beverages; state laws barring people from wearing religious garb in schools that received tax exemptions; and laws prohibiting the teaching of evolution, particularly in the South.

All this legislation represented a significant victory for the forces of fundamentalism, nativism, xenophobia, and moralism. Efforts to bring about such nativist and moralist restrictions have a long history going back almost to the beginning of the republic, but until the 1920s they achieved no widespread legislative success. Why should these crusades have won out in the 1920s? Why did the United States succumb at that time to a wave of repressive nationalist, moralistic, puritanical hysteria? There is no way, of course, to answer these questions with absolute certainty, but the analyses of this period by historians and social scientists suggest that these rightist actions represented the fear of many groups that persistent social change was finally destroying the kind of America they believed in, the Protestant culture in which they had been reared.

Perhaps the most palpable sign of such social change was the growth of the cities. The rural-urban rivalry cited earlier was made much more pointed by the rapidly increasing urbanization of the country. The 1920 census reported that for the first time the rural population had become a minority in the United States. The big cities were the centers of communications and of visible cultural influence. They were also the centers of settlement of the tremendous waves of immigrants who had come from the non-Protestant areas of Europe. Most of the immigration from the 1890s to World War I was Catholic, Orthodox Christian, or Jewish. Relatively little, proportionate to the total group, came from northern European Protestant countries. By World War I and after, this influx was reflected in the growing political power of Catholics through the urban Democratic machines, and in the power of the rising Jewish middle class. The cities which were dominating the economy and political life of the country seemed to be controlled by the large numbers of non-Protestant immigrants. The rapidly growing cities, of course, contained large numbers of Protestants, many of them workers who had migrated from rural areas. This group provided the Klan with a considerable low-status urban base which resented and resisted the political power of the urban Democratic machines, and the cultural liberalism of the urban cosmopolitan elites. Outside the urban areas, the Klan drew strength from evangelical Protestants living in the small towns and rural areas who began to feel that they were isolated provincials, far from the mainstream, while the cities were controlled by elites with different values, attitudes, and customs. As one Ku Klux Klan leader put it poignantly, "We have become strangers in the land of our fathers."

The pre-twentieth-century expressions of mass bigotry and belief in conspiracy theories had each arisen during periods marked by the sharp decline of the party supported by evangelical Protestants, Federalists, Whigs, and Republicans. Nineteen-twenty was also a year of drastic shift in party fortunes, but this time it was the Republican party which gained. The conservative restorative politics of Warren Harding were endorsed by over 60 per cent of the electorate, the largest percentage ever received by a Republican, while the incumbent Democrats fell to little more than one-third of the vote. Although the Klan in the North largely worked in and with the Republican party in many states, clearly partisan weakness was not a source of Klan strength. Rather it would appear that the rise of the Klan, the appeal of Henry Ford, and the massive increase in Republican support each reflected in a different way the desire of many Americans to restore an America changed by war, urbanization, and heavy waves of non-Nordic immigration, to reflect once more the values of a rural, moralistic, Protestant society.

The Republican party itself adapted to this shift in mood of its supporters. Campaigning for the presidency in 1920, Harding spoke of the dangers to America inherent in "racial differences," and recommended that the United States should only admit immigrants whose background indicated that they could develop "a full consecration to American practices and ideas." Shortly before the new administration took office in 1921, his vice president and successor as president, Calvin Coolidge, wrote that "biological laws show that Nordics deteriorate when mixed with other races." James J. Davis, Harding's and Coolidge's secretary of labor, went even further to argue for immigration restrictions on the ground that the older Nordic "immigrants to America were the beaver type who built up America, whereas the newer immigrants were rat-men trying to tear it down; and obviously rat-men could never become beavers." The third of the trio of Republican presidents of the twenties, Herbert Hoover, also joined in the chorus at the beginning of the decade when, speaking as secretary of commerce, he declared that "immigrants now lived in the United States on sufferance . . . and would be tolerated only if they behaved."

In reaction to a growing sense of displacement, the Protestant, nonmetropolitan Republicans of the North joined with the Protestant Democrats in the South against the big-city Democrats in the 1920s. This first Dixiecrat-Republican coalition led to the passage of prohibition, restrictions in immigration, and other repressive legislation already mentioned. Although their successes could be taken as indexes of the strength of these provincial and evangelical Protestant groups, it is probably more accurate to regard them as reflecting a backlash occurring at the very time when these interest groups were losing out. During the nineteenth century most Americans could have been described as white, Protestant, rural, small-town residents. Yet all during the time that they constituted an overwhelming majority, their more extreme beliefs—nativist, fundamentalist, prohibitionist—were not massively incorporated into legislation. It was only as the group was declining, as it began to see other groups and other values taking over, that the necessary impetus—in this case, fear—was provided to enact these values into law.

The rights of dissenters got short shrift during this period. On federal, state, and local levels, official actions limited the rights of political opposition through explicit legislation, legislative investigations, and administrative fiat. In the hunt for radicals, the Department of Justice was guilty of illegal search and seizure, of intimidating interrogation, of levying excessive bail, and of denial of counsel. Official action was matched by repressive private action, which included tarring and feathering, and in some instances lynching, political offenders. These offenders were typically regarded as being of the "wrong" color, the "wrong" religion, the "wrong" ethnic stock.

The hysteria of the twenties gradually died away. It died partly because, as in the case of the Klan, the causes which it espoused were relatively successful. It declined also because its excesses, its use of violence, led the more respectable elements who had either supported or tolerated it in its early period to drop away and help turn the fire of community social pressure on it. The Klan lost much of its middle-class support by 1924, and remained as a declining organization of less educated workers and farmers. It failed finally because these movements—like the APA and the Know-Nothings before it—were composed of extremists who tended to turn on each other in a bitter, aggressive, and paranoid way and thus to split up. The last gasp of the bigotry of the 1920s was the highly prejudicial anti-Catholic campaign against the presidential candidacy of Al Smith in 1928.

As in the case of the previous mass expressions of bigotry, the hysteria proved hard to maintain beyond a few years, but the legislation enacted during the twenties had long-lasting effects. Prohibition continued until 1933, with disastrous consequences for attitudes toward law and order. Biased immigration quotas lasted until just a few years ago. Although much of the politically restrictive legislation has been voided by the Supreme Court, some of it still remains on the books.

The decade of the thirties—with its massive economic depression, unemployment, and political pressures linked to revolutionary events in Europe—witnessed its share of extremist movements. Both left-wing and right-wing groups gained adherents in this difficult period. The list of rightist proto-Fascist movements is almost endless: the Silver Shirts of William Pelley, the Black Legion of the Midwest, the Christian Defenders of Gerald Winrod, the National Union for Social Justice of Father Charles Coughlin, the Committee of One Million of Gerald L. K. Smith, and so on. No one knows how many active members these groups had or how many others agreed with them.

Studies of the support of these groups indicate that they appealed heavily to the more religious, less educated, and more provincial elements among both Protestants and Catholics. Their conspiratorial charges were directed mainly against Jews and Communists but occasionally also against Catholics. Gerald Winrod, a principal Protestant fundamentalist figure, was pro-Nazi and virulently anti-Catholic and anti-Semitic. He was given to ominous warnings about the plots of the Elders of Zion.

The most important of these right-wing extremists was the Catholic priest, Charles Coughlin. The Coughlinite movement demonstrated that many Catholics could hate just as well as Protestants could. Openly anti-Semitic and increasingly pro-Fascist, Father Coughlin had an audience of millions for his weekly radio program. Reliable opinion polling, which began in the mid-thirties, showed that Coughlin's views were endorsed by more than 25 per cent of the adult population. His ideology sounded leftist to many, since he strongly opposed private ownership of the banks, and placed the responsibility for the depression on the desire for profit of international bankers, most of whom were identified as Jews.

It is interesting that both Winrod and Coughlin believed in the continued existence of the conspiracy of the Illuminati, that the same society which had supposedly organized the French Revolution had fostered the emergence of subsequent revolutionary movements, including the Russian Revolution, and now influenced the New Deal. Winrod, however, identified the Illuminati as the source of a Jesuit-Jewish alliance to dominate the world. Coughlin naturally did not speak of Catholic involvement, but he did link the Illuminati, and occasionally the Masons, with the efforts of the Elders of Zion and other Jewish groups, to advance communism.

The high point of Coughlin's support was attained early in 1936. His organization, the National Union for Social Justice, probably had close to a million members, with organized groups throughout most of the country. A much larger population listened sympathetically to his weekly radio broadcasts. Most congressional candidates endorsed by Coughlin in the 1936 primaries won their nomination fights. He disrupted the base of his support, however, by trying to turn his movement into a third party, the Union party, behind the presidential candidacy of William Lemke. By so doing, Coughlin ran into the perennial difficulty of such efforts, their inability to prevent sympathetic voters from backing the "lesser evil" between the two major party choices. In this case, many underprivileged Coughlinites who were benefiting from the extensive programs of the New Deal, chose to vote for Franklin Roosevelt. Lemke, who had the backing of 8 per cent of the electorate in July according to the Gallup Poll, wound up with less than 2 per cent of the vote. Coughlin, thereupon, dissolved his National Union organization and temporarily withdrew from politics. Although he returned soon after, forming new but much smaller organizations of supporters and voicing more explicit and virulent racist appeals, he never recovered from the failure of the Union party campaign.

In the latter years of the thirties, the Coughlinites and the myriad of other bigoted movements strongly opposed American intervention in World War II, since they tended to support the Nazis. Indeed, various opinion surveys indicate that close to half the population had strong anti-Semitic attitudes at a time when the Nazis were riding high in Europe. But the impact of Pearl Harbor, and in some cases direct government action, killed these movements during World War II.

Following the war, racial tensions and concern with communism supplanted anti-Catholicism and anti-Semitism as the most salient sources of conspiratorial belief. The major racist efforts in this postwar period date from the Supreme Court's desegregation decision in 1954. That decision prompted the formation of White Citizens' Councils and other groups aimed at throttling the struggle for Negro equality. The most prominent right-wing movement of the early fifties, however, was *not* racist. It was the anti-Communist movement spearheaded by Senator Joseph McCarthy which emerged in 1950. McCarthy tended to concentrate his attention on the conspiratorial sources of the failures of American foreign policy; these failures, he claimed, represented the work of undetected Communist agents who had infiltrated both the government and the key opinion-forming and policy-controlling institutions of the society. McCarthy alleged that these agents were particularly strong among the social elite—the graduates of Groton and Harvard, those who ran the newspapers, professors in the universities, the heads of the foundations, the personnel of the State Department, and so on. He thus appealed to the status strains of many socially and economically inferior segments of the society and transposed into a new key the conspiracy theme that has characterized so much of American extremist politics. Analysis of opinion-poll data bearing on support for McCarthy's activities indicated that it came disproportionately from the less privileged strata, especially those among his Catholic coreligionists, and from ethnic groups (German and Irish) and sections of the country (the Midwest particularly) which had been opposed to American entry into World War II.

Again typifying the conservative party's repeated reaction to extremist groups, many moderate leaders in the Republican party generally encouraged McCarthy before 1953, seeing in his activities an opportunity to win over the support of many underprivileged Democrats, particularly Catholics, who reacted strongly against the rise of communism abroad and the seeming decline of American world power. Richard Rovere has suggested that this behavior was a consequence of Republican reaction to Harry Truman's unanticipated victory over Thomas Dewey in the 1948 elections. Republican congressional triumphs in 1946, plus optimistic reports from the opinion polls, had led party leaders to anticipate that after sixteen years in opposition, they were about to take office. Defeat following on this sharp increase in their level of expectation undermined their commitment to the conventional rules of the political game, and led them, like the Federalists and Whigs earlier, to tolerate or encourage the use of extremist tactics. Victory in the 1952 elections ended their need to rely on such measures. McCarthy's insistence on continuing his attack against the governmental elite, now in the hands of Republicans, ultimately resulted in his censure in 1954 by the Senate. Thereafter, he almost totally disappeared from sight; the mass media, which had given extensive publicity to his attacks, simply stopped covering him. His public support, which also declined, may have been responding to these changes at the elite level, as well as to the end of the Korean War, which occurred about the same time.

After the McCarthy movement collapsed, a host of smaller right-wing groups emerged. Some of them have focused on the Jews and Communists and have charged that the civil rights movements and efforts to improve the situations of Negroes are part of a Jewish-Communist conspiracy. The most publicized movement of the sixties, the John Birch Society, has not been anti-Semitic, but it strongly opposes the civil rights movements. It has subscribed to conspiracy theory, identifying many of the economic and social trends which it opposes as a consequence of the efforts of a "hidden conspiracy of Insiders," that is, our old friends, the Illuminati. The Birch Society attributes both the rise of the welfare state and the growth of the civil rights movement to an alleged Illuminati-controlled Communist conspiracy.

In his pamphlet, *The Truth in Time,* Robert Welch credits the Illuminati with being responsible for both world wars, the Russian Revolution, the breakup of the colonial empires, the formation of the United Nations, centralized banking, the personal income tax, the direct election of senators in the United States, and "everything in the way of 'security' legislation, from the first Workmen's Compensation Acts under Bismarck to the latest Medicare monstrosity under Lyndon Johnson." Like Henry Ford, Welch sees continuity both in the conspiracy and in the opposition to it. Thus he identifies with the anti-Masonic movement of the early nineteenth century, stating that just as the Illuminati killed William Morgan, an opponent of Freemasonry whose kidnaping and disappearance in 1826 led to the formation of the anti-Masonic movement, they had also eliminated Senator Joseph McCarthy when he became aware of their activities.

Prejudice and Politics in America

In an unsigned introduction to a 1967 Birch Society edition of John Robison's book, *Proofs of a Conspiracy,* first published in 1798, the society makes clear who it thinks the Illuminati were and are:

This was a conspiracy conceived, organized and activated by professionals and intellectuals, many of them brilliant, but cunning and clever, who decided to put their minds in the service of total evil.... One tends to think of professors, philosophers and writers as sitting in their ivory towers, perfectly harmless to the world. Robison and history proved otherwise.... From Woodrow Wilson —himself a professor—to Lyndon Johnson, we have had nothing but Presidents surrounded by professors and scholars.... All of which brings to mind Weishaupt's plan to surround the ruling authorities with members of his Order.

And in discussing the current activities of the Illuminati, the Birch Society introduction states that they no longer use Freemasonry. "Their main habitat these days seems to be the great subsidized universities, tax-free foundations, mass media communication systems, and a myriad of private organizations, such as the Council on Foreign Relations."

The society, on the whole, eschews appeals to religious and racial bigotry, placing the brunt of its attack on the Illuminati and their Communist agents. It has expelled various members and some prominent leaders for anti-Semitic activities and statements. Although strongly against any efforts to foster civil rights or improve the socioeconomic conditions of the black population through governmental action, it seeks to find conservative Negroes whose activities it can identify with and support. The tenor of its attacks on the civil rights movement, however, frequently leads Birchers to write and speak about Negroes in terms which can only be described as racist. It also strongly supports the rights of white minorities to rule in South Africa and Rhodesia on the grounds that they constitute the only real alternative to communism or anarchy.

Given its strong ideological attack on all forms of the welfare state and trade unionism, the society has little or no appeal to the underprivileged. Analyses of the social composition of its membership, as well as of the 6 per cent or so of populations interviewed by opinion pollsters who are favorable to the Birch Society, indicate that it derives its support from a relatively affluent, well-educated stratum. Seemingly, according to studies of the society's membership by Fred Grupp, Murray Havens, and Burton Levy, they come from the less prestigious segment of the affluent, those who did not finish college, or who went to inferior ones. Their top leaders tend to be heads of family-owned corporations located in relatively small provincial cities. Like the APA and the Klan, Birch Society chapters are more likely to be found in rapidly expanding communities, particularly in the South and West.

The combination of deep conspiratorial and ultra-conservative dogma has meant that the organization has remained relatively small (possibly sixty thousand members at its height in 1965) and unpopular. Recognizing the difficulty of gaining wide support for its full program, Robert Welch, the founder and head of the society, has defined its role as that of a vanguard organization modeling its tactics on that of the Communists, that is, using "front organizations" in which Birch members can play controlling roles.

The largest and most important contemporary movement linked to racial concerns has been the American Independent party, headed by Governor George Wallace, who ran for President in 1968. Almost every extreme right-wing group, almost every virulent racist in the country, backed Wallace. He produced a coalition of the right such as probably never existed before, at least in the twentieth century. Birch Society members, in particular, played a leading role in the Wallace party and campaign organization in many states. In his 1964 campaign in the Democratic presidential primaries and in his later third-party effort, Wallace made strong pro-Birch Society statements. His campaign speeches were clear, simple, and insistent. Although he rarely mentioned Negroes as such, he campaigned strongly against government legislation which in any way involves enforcing integration or civil rights with respect to open housing, schools, unions, and so forth. He also spoke frequently about the need for force to deal with the breakdown in law and order, crime in the streets, and riots. Other frequent themes in his speeches dealt with fear of central government power generally and a concern for American weakness abroad, particularly as reflected in the inability to win in Vietnam.

Unlike the Birch Society, however, which is explicitly elitist, Wallace directed an appeal to the common man of America who, he has argued, is brighter and more moral than the elite. His heroes are the taxi driver, the steelworker, the auto mechanic, and the little man generally. He sees the "pseudo-intellectuals"—in the form of college professors, the heads of the "tax-free" foundations, editors of leading newspapers and magazines, members of the Council on Foreign Relations, and high-ranking bureaucrats in Washington—as the sources of evil and propagators of false doctrine. (The pseudo-intellectuals bear close resemblance to descriptions of the Illuminati in Birch Society literature.) Coming out of a southern Populist tradition, he suggests the existence of an elitist conspiracy based on the eastern establishment. Thus, during the campaign he argued that the public opinion polls were being deliberately manipulated against him by the "Eastern money interests." Taking a leaf out of Senator Joseph McCarthy's book, he has identified communism with the well-to-do rather than with the down-and-out, stating: "I don't believe all this talk about poor folks turning Communist. It's the damn rich who turn Communist. You ever seen a poor Communist?" Strongly antagonistic to the federal judiciary for its rulings on integration and on the rights of Communists and of defendants in criminal cases, Wallace proposed the plan first suggested by the Populists in the 1890s, the direct election of federal judges, a solution in line with his repeated emphasis on the moral and intellectual superiority of the common man.

Wallace's movement is not to be taken lightly. In the 1968 election Wallace received the support of 13.5 per cent of the electorate. His party was on the ballot in every state.

This is no mean accomplishment. It is certainly the first time in half a century that a third party has been on the ballot in every state, which shows the degree of organization and competency of this movement. The strength of Wallace's appeal was even greater than the vote he received indicates. Both the Gallup Poll and the Harris Poll reported at the end of September that 21 per cent of the electorate preferred him to Humphrey or Nixon. As election day approached, the Wallace support in the polls declined steadily as many of his supporters, recognizing that he could not win, began to feel the pressure to vote for the "lesser evil." Yet Wallace was able to retain more of his backing against such pressure than any other third-party candidate in almost half a century. And it should be noted that when the Gallup Poll inquired on a number of occasions in 1968, not how people intended to vote, but whether they approved or disapproved generally of George Wallace, more than 40 per cent indicated approval. But even granted that the election showing represents his full support—votes for Wallace are more than a minor following. Opinion polls since the election in 1969 and in 1970 report that he continues to maintain this backing.

Wallace finds his support in the same sorts of people sociologically as those who backed the earlier movements. They are disproportionately rural or small-town dwellers and Protestants (although he has considerable backing among Catholics). They are likely to be less educated and poorer than the population at large. Outside of white southern racist support, the largest segment of his backing in the 1968 election came from manual workers, many of them trade unionists. A special national poll of union members conducted by the Gallup organization for the *New York Times* early in October reported that 25 per cent of them supported Wallace. A referendum conducted within the United Automobile Workers among elected local and regional *officers* found over 10 percent choosing the American Independent party nominee. A number of trade union locals in the North actually endorsed his candidacy. Journalists reported deep concern on the part of union leaders concerning their membership's enthusiasm for Wallace. The very extensive campaign against Wallace waged by the unions succeeded in the North. He lost most of his union-member support by November, although it was still much higher (9 per cent) than among middle-class voters (4 per cent).

Many of these workers, who are steadily employed, are purchasing their own homes in neighborhoods which are relatively close to expanding black areas; bothered by higher taxes, they are opposed to the welfare program as a system which taxes the hard-working to help the lazy and unfit. To a considerable extent they identify these groups with the Negroes. Since white workingmen are much more likely to live inside the central cities than the more affluent middle class, they are also more directly and personally concerned with the problem of increased urban crime and with efforts at integrating urban school systems through modifying the concept of the neighborhood school. Many workers see the pressures for school desegregation as coming from the well-educated middle class, which lives in the suburbs or sends its children to private schools. The issue for them has become one of the well-to-do forcing the white working class to send its children to school with black children.

The disproportionate support given to George Wallace by American workers—a phenomenon akin to the backing received by the Know-Nothings, the APA, the Ku Klux Klan, the Coughlinite Christian Front, and Senator Joseph McCarthy—contradicts the assumption of many who identify the working class and trade unionism with support for progressive social objectives. This phenomenon of working-class endorsement for bigotry *and* for trade unionism and the welfare state coincides with the results of various sociological surveys which have found that the less educated (and, therefore, also poorer) people are, the more likely they are to be prejudiced against minority groups, and to be intolerant of deviance generally. Conversely, however, the less well-to-do a group, the more disposed it is to favor liberal-left policies with regard to issues such as the position of trade unions, social security, economic planning, and the like. Workers and the less affluent generally vote for liberal-left parties because they see these parties as defenders of their economic and class interests against the conservatives who are identified in their minds with the well-to-do and big business. A candidate who seeks to appeal to their racial sentiments, but is also visibly opposed to their economic interests, such as Barry Goldwater in 1964, cannot gain their votes.

George Wallace, however, shied away from such positions, and sought to identify the pressures for Negro equality and integration with the eastern establishment and the intellectual elite. Not being a Republican also probably helped his image with many workers. They can more easily vote for a candidate and party which appeals to the common man than for a candidate and party which they identify with the wealthy. And Wallace did make a direct appeal for such support on economic lines by calling for a sharp increase in social security payments and for doubling the personal exemption on the income tax, a change which would particularly benefit the less affluent. His party platform also proposed liberalizing payments under the Medicare program. It may be significant to note that the Harris Poll reported that many more Wallace supporters in the North chose the term "radical" to describe his political outlook than described him as a "conservative."

Not surprisingly, the opinion polls indicated that Wallace supporters in the North tended to come from Democratic ranks (and those who abandoned Wallace before election day seemed to have voted for Hubert Humphrey). The opinion analyst, Samuel Lubell, reported in late October that "Pro-Wallace supporters in the northern cities . . . voice strong working-class views which prevent them from voting Republican. . . . Most of these Wallace followers maintain, 'Wallace is for the workingman. He couldn't be for anyone else.' Some even talk of the Wallace movement as 'the start of a new labor party.' "

One relatively low-status occupation group which has been

reported as heavily involved in the ranks of Wallace supporters is policemen. In this respect also the American Independent party resembles its predecessors on the extreme right. Data bearing on the membership of the American Protective Association in the 1890s, of the Ku Klux Klan of the twenties and fifties, of the Black Legion and the Coughlinite Christian Front of the thirties, and of the Birch Society in the sixties, have indicated the disproportionate presence of policemen in their ranks. A number of elements in their social background and work experience predisposes them to racial bigotry. As Gunnar Myrdal noted almost three decades ago, policemen tend to be recruited from the lower-status and less-educated segments of the population. A recent study of the New York police describes the typical recruit as being of "working-class background, high school education or less, average intelligence, cautious personality." Prejudice against Negroes is greater among persons with such backgrounds. Police work tends to reinforce and intensify such feelings, since it brings policemen into contact with the worst elements in the Negro community.

The policeman's role is also particularly subject to creating feelings of resentment against society flowing from status discrepancies. On one hand, he is given considerable authority by society to enforce its laws and is expected to risk his life if necessary; on the other, he receives little prestige and a relatively low salary. A number of studies of police report a common complaint that they are not respected by the public. And overt hostility and even contempt for the police often are voiced by spokesmen for liberal and left groups, and intellectuals. Insofar as the police find any segment of the body politic showing appreciation for their contribution to society, and for the risks they take, it is from conservatives, and particularly from the far right. Thus, the slogan "Support Your Local Police" was enunciated by the Ku Klux Klan in the early twenties, revived by the Birch Society in the sixties, and placed on the automobile license plates of the state of Alabama by George Wallace when he was governor. The Birch Society has established awards for heroic policemen and has set up a fund for the support of the families of police killed in the line of duty. George Wallace went out of his way in campaign speeches to praise the police and to denounce their liberal intellectual critics.

Within the strata which disproportionately backed George Wallace, young people have been prevalent. Gallup and Harris surveys reported in October, 1968, that 25 per cent —one out of every four—between twenty-one and twenty-nine years old were for Wallace, as contrasted with 20 per cent among the older groups. These age differences were even more pronounced in the actual voting, especially in the North.

It is interesting to note that this phenomenon of disproportionate youth support for an extremist racist candidate has largely been ignored by those who have identified young America with left-wing campus demonstrators and student volunteers for Robert Kennedy and Eugene McCarthy. In a real sense, the New Right of George Wallace, like the New

Left, is a direct outgrowth of a process of political polarization which emerged around the efforts to secure desegregation from the late fifties on. Many of the liberal white university students who joined the civil rights movement began to despair of American democracy when they witnessed authority in the South violating the law in order to preserve segregation. The tactics of civil disobedience and sit-ins first emerged among the student left as a response to the civil disobedience initiated by such white segregationist leaders as Ross Barnett of Mississippi, Lester Maddox of Georgia, and George Wallace of Alabama. At the same time, however, many white youths in the South and in the urban working-class areas of the North had grown up during a period in which the issue of integration within their schools and communities had been salient. They were reared in an atmosphere in which the voicing of anti-Negro sentiments in their homes and neighborhoods was common, in which members of the older generation discussed their fears concerning the adverse consequences of school or residential integration. Hence, while the upper-middle-class scions of liberal parents were being radicalized to the left, southern and northern working-class youth were being radicalized to the right. The consequences of such polarization can be seen in the behavior of the two groups in the 1968 election campaign.

The indications that the Wallace movement draws heavily among youth are congruent with the evidence from various studies of youth and student politics that young people are disposed to support the more extreme or idealistic version of the politics dominant within their social group. In Europe, radical movements, both of the left and of the right, have been much more likely to secure the backing of the young than the democratic parties of the center. Being less committed to existing institutions and parties than older people, being less inured to the need to compromise to achieve objectives, youth are attracted to movements and leaders who promise to resolve basic problems quickly in an absolute fashion. Unfortunately, as yet few data exist that bear on the extent to which the earlier American rightist movements also drew from youth.

The conclusion that concern over race and the related issues of "law and order" was the dominant sentiment among Wallace voters was borne out by the national opinion surveys. The pollster Louis Harris reported:

The common bond that sews together this unusual assortment of political allies in this election is dominantly race. A heavy 73 per cent of all Wallace supporters want progress for Negroes to be halted. Almost as many, 67 per cent, say that they "feel uneasy personally due to the prospect of race riots in their own community."

Feeling about racial issues is, of course, not the only factor which has fostered the emergence of a New Right. The Wallace movement has disproportionate support among farmers and residents of small towns, who are rarely in contact with the Negroes. Many in these groups appear to be responding to a concern over the changes in American religious and cultural beliefs. They are often religious or secular fundamentalists. They oppose changes in that old-time religion and in the traditional American individualist way of life. The religious fundamentalists, concentrated in rural areas and small towns, or among migrants from such places to big cities, feel deprived by the fact that American society has become cosmopolitan and metropolitan. Fundamentalist values are treated as provincial and anachronistic by those who control the mass media and the cultural life of the nation. These cultural trends, of course, have intensified with the passage of time, and to a considerable extent now dominate the major theological tendencies within both Protestantism and Catholicism. This group of traditionalist Christians, now definitely a minority, has become a principal source of support for a politics of alienation and nostalgia. And to the resentments of the religious fundamentalists are joined those of many not particularly religious people who are deeply disturbed by changes in secular values.

It should be noted, however, that except among the minority of committed extremists, the Wallace movement as such failed to make headway with the bulk of affluent and better-educated upper- and middle-class conservatives. In mid-October, 1968, the *New York Times* conducted a national opinion survey of the presidents of *all* the companies whose shares are listed in the New York Stock Exchange, using the anonymous questionnaire technique. The survey indicated that less than half of 1 per cent (three men) were for Wallace, whereas 85 per cent endorsed Richard Nixon, and

13 per cent backed Hubert Humphrey. Although Wallace had more support in lower levels of the business and professional community, particularly in the South, it is clear from the polls that the top level was disproportionately opposed to him. Most of these people, though economic conservatives, are not afraid that the country is being taken over by Negroes or other minority groups and are not alienated from the body politic. Insofar as they are politically motivated, they are active in the Republican party. In California they united in 1966 behind Ronald Reagan, who embodies these conservative virtues. On a local and congressional level they could find many candidates with kindred opinions within the GOP in 1968. Richard Nixon, who supported Goldwater in 1964 and who in turn was strongly supported by him before the Republican convention in 1968, though not as conservative as some of them would like, still was sufficiently close to such views to retain their support.

The Wallace movement clearly is not a conservative tendency. Rather, it is a movement of the alienated adherents of religious and secular fundamentalism. It appeals to those who really feel threatened by the rise of the Negro in the cities, by the changes in the moral order which they can witness nightly on television, by the changing content of Protestantism and Catholicism, by miniskirts, and by the decline of the United States on the world scene. There are many such frustrated individuals in America today. George Wallace has found a way of reaching many of them. In a real sense, he is trying to build a Poujadist movement out of those who reject "modernism."

The reactionary movements of the 1960s—the Wallace movement, the Birch Society, the Christian Crusade of Billy James Hargis, and others—resemble the backlash politics that swept the country in the 1920s. Today, as in the twenties, many continue to be out of step with the dominant cultural trends of the society and to feel bitter about the decline of traditional Christian morality. It remains to be seen how powerful they will be this time. On the one hand their base in fundamentalists living in small towns and rural areas no longer constitutes the near-majority it did in the 1920s; now it represents only a small minority. But on the other hand this group has been joined by the scions of the immigrants in the large cities, many of them Catholics, threatened by the inroads made by Negroes. Many of them react today to the growth in urban Negro population much as white Protestant workers reacted to the Catholic immigration in the nineteenth century.

The racial resentments of the provincial fundamentalist Protestants, including many who have moved to large cities, and of the children of immigrants are playing a major role in the realignment of American politics occurring in the 1960s. Once again their resentments are contributing to the ranks of the more conservative of the two major parties as well as making possible the rise of parties and movements with explicit racial orientations. The fears of these people have been expressed in recent years by many mayoral candidates, such as Louise Day Hicks in Boston, Charles Stenvig in Minneapolis, or Sam Yorty in Los Angeles, as well as by a number of prominent right-wing Republicans who have appealed to racism indirectly by discussing the dangers of crime in the streets, riots, or open-housing legislation. Clearly, though many of them have not openly talked about Negroes and race, they can say, as Mrs. Hicks did, "You know where I stand."

Once again it must be said that a leader of the Republicans, Richard Nixon, has sought to refurbish the strength of his party among traditional Democratic supporters by appealing to those who have shown a readiness to abandon their party allegiance in favor of a racist candidate. As the *New York Times* reported,[3] using "the Wallace slogan, 'Stand up for America,' he lauds Senator Strom Thurmond [the presidential candidate of an earlier effort to create a third pro-segregationist party in 1948] as a man 'who has stood up for his state and will stand up for America and I'm glad to stand with him today.' " Many analysts of the 1968 election have described the campaign tactics of the Republican vice-presidential candidate, Spiro Agnew, as an effort to "out-Wallace Wallace." He spoke out repeatedly in strong terms about the need to crack down on threats to law and order, explained the fact that he did not campaign in Negro areas by saying "if you've seen one ghetto area, you've seen them all," described Hubert Humphrey as "soft on Communism," and

[3] October 12, 1968, p. 10E.

attacked "phony intellectuals [Wallace's favorite target] who don't understand what we mean by hard work and patriotism." Since Agnew maintained his Wallace-like posture throughout the campaign, there can be little doubt that he was fulfilling a role assigned to him by party strategists, that is, showing Wallace supporters that they could get what they wanted from the Republican party. In the year and a half since the election, Agnew has continued the same approach. Wallace himself has complained that the Republicans are "copy-cats," that he should have copyrighted his speeches to prevent their being plagiarized by the Vice-President. Thus, the major consequence of the Wallace movement may be that it, like the Anti-Masonic and the Know-Nothing American parties, will serve as a transmission belt to bring the more bigoted Democrats to the opposition conservative party which adapts its policies to accommodate their concerns.

There is some danger, however, that George Wallace may try to mobilize his supporters in a new mass movement which, like some of the earlier ones, will engage in extra-parliamentary confrontationist tactics, including taking to the streets to intimidate opponents. During the campaign he openly discussed the possibility of a "white revolution" should he fail to win, directed toward forcing the state governments "to physically take over the schools" to end integration. As he described the process, there would first be mass rallies and protest demonstrations throughout the country. The vigor of such protests would press the states to bring about a halt in federal interference in local school policies.

Wallace has argued that the common people are ready for drastic action, and boasts of the fact that many in his campaign audiences became hysterical when he discussed law and order and school integration. In the spring of 1970 he began to call for direct action to stop bussing and other integration measures. Clearly, Wallace has been toying with the idea of turning his electoral party into a mass movement which will take to the streets to counter the activities of the "anarchists," the demonstrations and riots in the ghettoes and on the campuses. The implications of such an endeavor for the future of democratic politics in the United States are obvious.

As a final evaluative point, it is important to recognize that all of the earlier movements discussed here have been short-lived, even though most of them involved millions of people in their activities. Various analysts have explained their rise as a result of basic endemic tension-creating processes, explanations which imply that some of them should have survived for much longer than they did, since the conditions which supposedly gave rise to them continued while the movements declined or died. Thus, the heyday of the Anti-Masons was from 1828 to 1832. The Know-Nothing American party was able to win elections in many states from 1854 to 1857, but quickly dwindled away thereafter. The American Protective Association became a multi-million member alliance in 1892–94, but disintegrated by 1896. The Ku Klux Klan presumably recruited close to four million members between 1921 and 1924, and helped elect many governors and other officials. It was an important force at both major party national conventions in 1924. By 1925 it had lost much of its membership, and by the late twenties it was a small group. The two largest movements of the 1930s, which had considerable support according to the opinion polls, were Huey Long's Share-Our-Wealth movement and the Coughlinite organizations. Long's movement, which was formed in 1934, totally vanished with his assassination in 1935: his second-in-command, Gerald L. K. Smith, could not find a handful to follow him. Coughlin's high point with respect to membership and popular support occurred in 1936. Thereafter, he led a declining movement, which disappeared into limbo after Pearl Harbor. The phenomenon known as McCarthyism lasted four years, from 1950 to 1954.

Looking over this record suggests the need not only to determine the conditions under which different groups of Americans become disposed to form and join movements which are far outside of the American "consensus," but also why they decline so quickly. Some of them, for example, the Anti-Masons and possibly the Ku Klux Klan, lost out after seemingly achieving their most prominent objectives. Others, like the APA, the Klan, and McCarthy, lost strength after being deserted by segments of the more established elements which had supported them in their early period. This came about either because the moderates had achieved some of "their" objectives—that is, the political defeat of their opponents—or because the extremist tactics of the movements make it difficult for respectable individuals to remain identified with them. Some, like the Know-Nothings and the APA, splintered because they included many who differed widely on issues other than the main one which brought them into existence. A few, particularly the Klan, have declined after revelations that their leaders were involved in fraudulent activities, or had begun to fight among themselves.

Although no one has presented an adequate general explanation for the short-lived character of American protest movements, a few statements can be made. First, those which have tried the "third party" route have been unable to break through the constraints placed on such efforts by the American constitutional structure, which makes of the entire country one constituency for the one important election, that of the presidency. Like the Know-Nothings in 1856 and the Coughlinites in 1936, they wind up in presidential elections with much less support than they had previously. One of the major parties usually makes some efforts to appeal to their supporters, and many of them vote for the "lesser evil" on election day. The movements, as distinct from the parties, often attract leaders and activists, whose values and personalities make it difficult for them to compromise on new issues facing the group. The intense factional struggles which often arise result in such acrimonious bickering as to discourage many of their members and supporters. Those movements which become more extreme in their tactics often find the moderate groups withdrawing. The establishment—in the form of the media, community, church, and political leaders—ultimately unites against extremist movements which show a capacity to survive and places them outside the pale of socially tolerated activity. But whatever the cause of decline, the fact remains that all such extremist efforts have quickly subsided. And although the social strains which led millions to join or follow these movements presumably continued to exist, efforts to continue or revive them once the process of decline has started, have invariably failed. There is no secular tendency connected with any of them.

This concludes a brief analysis of the appeals that have been made to racial and religious prejudice in efforts to preserve the status or values of groups with a prior claim to the American tradition. The story has been discouraging, but this does not mean that no changes occur. On the positive side one may point to the fact that overt support for bigotry has become much more shamefaced than in the past. No prominent American politician speaks directly about the negative traits of minority groups in the way that leading Whigs and Republicans did in the nineteenth and early twentieth centuries. Lest we forget, it should be noted again that the Republican presidents of the 1920s—Harding, Coolidge, and Hoover—all openly spoke or wrote about the threat to American values posed by Americans of non-Anglo-Saxon backgrounds. Except in the South, no politician dares any longer to attack Negroes by name. Racist appeals of course continue, but they now take the form of discussion of the "problems" created by unspecified groups. To the inhabitants of the ghetto such changes may seem trivial, when men can still get elected by appealing to the fears and bigotry of whole sections of the population. Yet the fact that the major party politicians who speak of the problems of law and order also feel obliged to advance a program which is ostensibly designed to improve economic and educational conditions in the ghetto, does attest to an improvement in the attitudes of white America. All the opinion polls agree that there has been a decline in expressed antiminority attitudes, whether these be toward Negroes, Catholics, or Jews. It is striking to note, for example, that the religious affiliation of Robert Kennedy and Eugene McCarthy was never mentioned during the 1968 campaign.

Given the existence of institutionalized sources of discrimination, such change in attitudes implies no more than unrealized potential. American institutions are still fundamentally biased in favor of whites, but Americans as a people are closer to expressing a belief in the American creed of equality than they have ever been. Whether they believe in it deeply enough to live by it is another question. The struggle for a genuinely equalitarian society is obviously far from having been won. There will be many reversals, but the long-term direction of the change remains consistent. Unfortunately, the pace of change is slow relative to needs. Thus one can still safely predict that if we all come together a decade or two hence to discuss patterns of prejudice there will be plenty of new evidence of the propensity of Americans to organize to suppress others because of their racial, religious, or ethnic traits.

There is, of course, the additional problem posed by race. The fact that race is such a visible characteristic, the fact that

Prejudice and Politics in America

Negroes cannot become physically indistinguishable from other Americans simply by virtue of changes in their educational and occupational status—this undoubtedly means that racial prejudice is going to be much more difficult to eradicate than religious or ethnic prejudices. But one observation about political institutions can give us some encouragement: the political system not only functions as an arena within which religious or racial tensions can be expressed; it also serves as the avenue through which minority groups have gained first symbolic and later real power and status. Parties have nominated and elected members of minority groups which have been disliked by the great majority in order to gain the votes of the minority. As Gunnar Myrdal pointed out a quarter of a century ago, many politicians who are personally prejudiced often have supported measures fostering equality. Electing blacks to high office is an excellent way to improve the status of a group traditionally stereotyped as lowly. Hence, in addition to measures directly concerned with improving the educational and economic situations of the black population, it is important that both major parties be pressed to nominate and help elect black leaders. In this way a new and much more hopeful chapter can be written in the doleful history of politics and prejudice.

As a final note on the politics of prejudice, it is important to recognize that right-wing political protest in America has almost invariably taken on an anti-elitist and often specifically anti-intellectual cast. In spite of the fact that such movements are seeking to preserve existing privileges and traditional values, they reflect the deep commitment to egalitarianism with the concomitant anti-elitism inherent in the American value system. When bigoted movements attacked Catholics and Jews in the past, they did so in part by identifying these groups with positions of political, economic, and cultural power. The Catholic danger to America was supposedly a result of a deliberate conspiracy by the Catholic hierarchy and the Pope, in league with Catholic politicians, to take over America and subject it to their European elitist structure and values. The Jewish threat was identified with the dire activities of international bankers. Even communism must be presented as a threat flowing from within the elite, not from the poor. And when ethnic elites have not been available as a target, the focus of hostility has been directed against the Illuminati as the surrogate for the intellectuals.

The current upsurge of anti-intellectualism expressed by the Wallace movement has repeated the oldest populist American conspiracy theme, that which identifies changes in values and institutions with the deliberate subversive efforts of the intellectual elite. The Negroes, on the other hand, cannot be and are not identified as part of the elite. They, therefore, are not the real villains; rather they are perceived as pawns manipulated by the Illuminati, the Communists, or the intellectuals to achieve their subversive ends. Those involved in anti-civil rights movements can, therefore, honestly feel that they are not racists, that they are not anti-Negro. The poor Negro who seeks to move out of the ghetto, who desires to put his child in an integrated school, who presses on white unions for membership, is only a weak tool, more to be pitied than hated. That the Birch Society, the Christian Crusade, or the American Independent party focus their resentments on intellectuals rather than Negroes does not make the situation of the Negroes any better. It does point up, however, how the stress on racial and religious bigotry in America may decline at the same time that extremist movements designed to protect white supremacy and fundamentalist values are fostered. The enemy in America must always be associated with the elite, never with the common man, whether he be black or white.

Biological Determinants of Individuality

RENÉ DUBOS

MY COLLEAGUES have been speaking of political man, social man, man in the abstract. I wish to speak of the man of flesh and bone.

DETERMINISTIC ASPECTS OF INDIVIDUALITY

All human beings are related, biologically and mentally, but no two of them have exactly the same biological and mental constitution. Furthermore, the individuality of any person living now is different from that of anyone who has ever lived in the past or will live in the future. Each person is unique, unprecedented, and unrepeatable.

Individuality is partly of genetic origin. Except for identical twins, no two persons inherit the same array of genes. Furthermore, the statistical chance is practically nil that the array of genes possessed by a given person today has ever occurred in the past, or will ever occur again. But individuality also results from the fact that each person has been

Biological Determinants of Individuality

conditioned by the unique constellation of surroundings and events that have influenced his development. Most of the stimuli that impinge on a person leave a stamp that cannot be eradicated and that conditions all his subsequent responses to other stimuli. Behavioral patterns and emotional attitudes, just like immunities and allergies, can be regarded as different forms of biological memory which persist in the organism through most or all of its life.

Conditioning by the environment begins during the intrauterine life. Even though the Dionne quintuplets were genetically identical, they could be differentiated by their attendants from the time of birth, and their biological and mental individualities became increasingly different as they grew older. It is probable that the relative position of the five fetuses in the uterus created for each of them slightly different environmental conditions at critical stages of their development, thus resulting in phenotypic distinctiveness. Much evidence is now accumulating that prenatal influences—as exerted, for example, by nutritional and hormonal factors, let alone by drugs and infectious agents—exert on the fetus profound effects that persist after birth and throughout life.

As commonly used by Watsonian behaviorists and Freudian psychoanalysts, the phrase "early influences" denotes the conditioning of emotional and mental characteristics by the forces that impinge on the newborn baby and on the child during the formative stages of his development, especially as a result of parental child-rearing practices. There are, however, many other kinds of environmental forces that play important roles in shaping individuality by acting on the organism early in its life and thus imposing directions and limitations to its development. From topography of the land to climatic factors, from nutrition to education, from sensual stimuli to religious beliefs—countless are the types of influences that leave a permanent stamp on the developing organism.

Early experiences do more than condition behavioral patterns and emotional attitudes. They also affect profoundly and lastingly other biological characteristics, such as initial growth rate, efficiency in the utilization of food, anatomic structures, physiologic attributes, maximum adult size, response to various forms of stresses and stimuli, in brief almost every phenotypic expression of the adult.

Granted that early influences—both prenatal and postnatal—play the most important role in converting genetic potentialities into the biological and mental attributes by which we know a person, it is also true that surroundings and events continue to have formative effects on the adult throughout his life span. Responses made by the adult organism to environmental stimuli can also become inscribed in the body and the mind, thereby altering subsequent responses to the same and other stimuli.

Individuality therefore reflects the evolutionary past of the person as encoded in this genetic apparatus and the experiential past as inscribed in the bodily structures that store biological and mental memory. It always takes forms that are conditioned by the past.

Biological Determinants of Individuality

Since individuality includes at any given time all the inherited potentialities that have been made functional by the life experiences of the person, and since it is continually changing in response to environmental stimuli, it might be defined as the evolving phenotype. One might also say that it incarnates the past.

FREE WILL AND INDIVIDUALITY

The awareness of personal freedom in making decisions is a straightforward experience which appears incompatible with the deterministic view of behavior discussed in the preceding section. In fact, when the process of decision-making is analyzed in all its details, step by step, freedom seems to disappear because all aspects of behavior are found to be under the control of genetic, experiential, and environmental factors.

Attempts to find a theoretical formulation that would accommodate both determinism and free will have so far failed. This is not surprising because the history of science shows that complex phenomena are rarely explainable in terms of concepts derived from studies of simpler and more restricted systems. Light cannot be understood by regarding it merely as a stream of particles moving in accordance with the classical laws of mechanics. Similarly, it is improbable that the experience of free will can be explained by the contemporary concepts of physics, chemistry, and natural selection which are presently used to account for gross biological phenomena.

RENÉ DUBOS

Niels Bohr saw in the determinism-freedom polarity a biological manifestation of the complementarity principle he had formulated for subatomic processes. Just as physicists study the electron either as a wave or as a particle, depending upon the conditions under which its behavior is observed, so Bohr suggested that human behavior should be studied as a manifestation either of free will or of determinism, depending upon the point of view of the observer. In this essay, I shall accept free will as a needed and useful belief, even though I do not know how to account for it—simply because I consider the experience of freedom more impressive than the failure to prove its existence.

Operationally, the manifestations of free will can be recognized at several levels of complexity.

All observers of animal life acknowledge the impossibility of predicting with certainty the behavior of a given animal in a given situation. Pavlov himself emphasized that even his best conditioned dogs often failed to behave according to prediction. This unpredictability of response led an exasperated physiologist to state what has come to be known as "The Harvard Law of Animal Behavior": "Under precisely controlled conditions, an animal does as he damn pleases." The same law applies with even greater strength to all human beings.

During the first few years of his life, the human child becomes aware of his environment, stores information about it, and develops almost passively certain patterns of responses. This phase of biological maturation is followed by a

Biological Determinants of Individuality

more active and conscious one during which the child appears to try to create his individuality by making use of his genetic endowment and early experiences.

During mid-childhood—perhaps after the age of five—the child tries to imagine, out of the information and patterns of responses acquired almost passively, a world of his own in which he can act out his individuality. I have used here the word "imagine" in the sense given it by Shelley in "Defence of Poetry." "We want the creative faculty to imagine [that is, create an image of] that which we know." Most of subsequent life consists in the unfolding of the behavior patterns that are elicited by this imagined world, in which biological constitution and environmental forces are inextricably woven.

In normal human beings, an increasing degree of individual freedom in making decisions is evidence of continuing development. Adult man is par excellence the creature who can eliminate, choose, organize, and thereby create. His individuality becomes richer and more complex as he responds to environmental forces and takes initiatives according to certain values and anticipations of the future that are largely his creations, yet have their roots in his past.

Much of the modern existentialist literature is an affirmation of the person's right to affirm his individuality at the moment of action. In fact, this right had been proclaimed with passion by many influential writers of the past century. For example:

Fyodor Dostoevski: "Man only exists for the purpose of

proving to himself that he is a man and not an organ-stop. He will prove it even if it means physical suffering, even if it means turning his back on civilization."

Jose Ortega y Gasset: "Living is precisely the inexorable necessity to make oneself determinate, *to enter into an exclusive destiny,* to accept it—that is, to resolve to *be it.* We have, whether we like it or not, to realize our 'personage,' our vocation, our vital program, our 'entelechy'—there is no lack of names for the terrible reality which is our authentic I (ego)."

André Gide: "What could have been said by someone other than you, do not say it; what could have been done by someone other than you, do not do it; of yourself, be interested only in those aspects that do not exist except in you; create out of yourself, patiently or impatiently, the most unique and irreplaceable of beings."

Paul Tillich: "Individualism is the self-affirmation of the individual self as individual self without regard to its participation in its world."

In the practical experience of daily life, the expressions of individuality reflect a functioning structure made up of inherited and acquired characteristics that are organically integrated. This integrated structure is more or less enduring and remains effective long after the conditions that have brought it into being have disappeared. Since each person is characterized by such a unique structure which is largely of his own making, his responses to environmental stimuli acquire a certain degree of independence from his evolutionary past and even from the culture to which he belongs. Irrespective of theories concerning the ultimate nature of free will, this independence is operationally the attribute that enables man to create a future of his own choice.

Each manifestation of free will selects a set of conditions under which the organism operates and which thereby influences his further development by eliciting responses that become lastingly incorporated in his physical and mental constitution. More importantly perhaps, decisions that affect the total environment condition the responses and development of young people exposed to this environment during the formative stages of their life.

Each individual decision thus imposes a direction and a pattern on the future development of the person and of his social group. In this sense, man makes himself, individually and socially, through a continuous series of responsible choices governed by anticipations of the future and value judgments.

ENVIRONMENTAL DETERMINANTS OF FREEDOM

As is the case for other potentialities of man's nature, the actualization of free will has deterministic components. Free will can express itself in acts of freedom only when conditions are favorable. For example, slum children are almost denied the chance to actualize their human potentialities. It is not correct to say that lack of culture determines their behavior. The more painful truth is that they acquire early in life a slum culture from which they are almost unable to escape.

Their early surroundings and ways of life limit the range of manifestations of their free will and thus destroy much of their potential freedom.

In the words of J. B. S. Haldane, "That society enjoys the greatest amount of liberty in which the greatest number of human genotypes can develop their peculiar abilities. It is generally admitted that liberty demands equality of opportunity. It is not equally realized that it demands a variety of opportunities." The phrase "variety of opportunities" is usually given a broad political and sociological interpretation. But it implies also precise biological determinants of behavior.

Experiments in animals, and observations in man, have revealed that the development of the brain, of learning ability, and of behavioral attitudes, is conditioned by the metabolic factors that affect anatomic and physiological growth, and by the sensual stimuli to which the organism is exposed. An impoverished environment results almost inevitably in biological and mental deficiency.

Since human potentialities can be realized only to the extent that circumstances favor their phenotypic expression, diversity within a given culture is an essential component of true functionalism. The latent potentialities of human beings have a better chance to emerge as living expressions when the social environment is sufficiently diversified to provide a variety of stimulating experiences, especially for the young.

As more and more persons find it possible to express their biologic endowments under a variety of conditions, society becomes richer and civilizations continue to unfold. In contrast, if the surroundings and ways of life are highly stereotyped—whether in prosperity or in poverty—the only components of man's nature that flourish are those adapted to the narrow range of prevailing conditions. Hence, the dangers of the typical modern housing developments which, although sanitary and comfortable, are designed as if their only function was to provide disposable cubicles for dispensable people.

Irrespective of their genetic constitution, most young people raised in a featureless environment, and limited to a narrow range of life experiences, will be crippled intellectually and mentally. For this reason, we must shun uniformity of surroundings as much as absolute conformity in behavior. Creating diversified environments may result in some loss of efficiency, but diversity is vastly more important than efficiency because it is essential to the germination of the seeds dormant in man's nature.

Since the physical and social environment plays a crucial role in the exercise of freedom, the objectives of environmental design should be to provide conditions for enlarging as much as possible the range of choices. The word "design" as used here applies to social planning, urban or rural development, and all the practices that affect the conduct of life. In a larger sense, it refers also to problems of values, for free will can operate only where there is first some form of conviction.

Values are often considered unchangeable because they are built in man's innate ethical nature. In practice, however, many of the values by which men operate are based on prevailing social attitudes as well as on inclinations, prejudices, and common sense derived from the experience of daily life. There is also a real possibility that, in the future, values might increasingly originate from the natural and social sciences—provided scientists make it their business to be concerned with values as well as with things. Scientific knowledge per se cannot define or impose values to govern behavior, but it provides a factual basis for option.

While choice can be made more rational by basing it on factual information, and on evaluation of consequences, it always retains a personal component because it must ultimately involve a value judgment. This ambiguous phrase constitutes another way of expressing the determinism-freedom polarity, which is one of the most characteristic aspects of the human condition.

Freedom is concerned not only with what to do, but even more perhaps with what not to do. It does not imply anarchy and complete permissiveness, since some form of discipline is essential to the integration of human as well as animal societies. Total rejection of discipline is unbiologic and would inevitably result in the disintegration of individual lives and of the social order. It is incompatible with physical, mental, and social health, indeed with the survival of the human species.

Design, rather than anarchy, is the characteristic of life. In human life, design implies the acceptance and even the deliberate choice of certain constraints which are deterministic to the extent that they incorporate the past and the influences of the environment. But design is also the expression of free will governed by value judgments and anticipations of the future.

Concluding Remarks

ABRAHAM KAPLAN

When I listened to the individual presentations and the panel's discussions of them, I was struck by the great variety of our different treatments of the same subject matter. I enjoyed having the freedom to express my own individuality. As I experienced the results of the same freedom enjoyed by the other participants, however, and faced the increasingly difficult task of finding some unities in the pluralities with which they were confronting me, there was a significant change in my attitudes toward both freedom and individuality (to say nothing of my attitudes toward the members of the panel themselves!).

The observation provides us with the first point to be noted in a résumé of this conference on individuality. Even with as much in common as there has been in the environments of the participants, and in the values which we have been conditioned to acknowledge, we still exhibit a considerable range of individual differences. It is noteworthy, too,

Concluding Remarks

from the very outset, that individuality can be both encouraged and restrained by forces not entirely in the control of the individual.

On the psychological side of our subject, one of the recurrent themes of our discussions has been the process of growth of individuality in the young, and their experience of the gap between the generations. For my part, I am able to view the generation gap with a certain equanimity—not because of what is called philosophic detachment, but because I continually remind myself that inevitably the members of the younger generation will themselves become over forty, and so presumably will turn into scoundrels like the rest of us.

As I listened to Keniston's summary of the attitudes of some of the fringe groups among the young, I thought of the many criticisms of them made by editors, clergymen, generals, and politicians—by all four Estates, in fact. The faults usually attributed to the young are those for which we used to have a simple expression: we called it being sophomoric. What else are we to expect of sophomores?

In the panel discussion, the question was put to Dr. Dubos whether it is possible ever to become fully mature; he answered the question brilliantly. I thought of another reply, in some lines written long ago which strongly anticipate the ideas of Freud and other scientists concerned with the process of growth; they appear in the Prologue to Goethe's *Faust:* "Tis not that we leave childhood as we age, but that we learn at last what children we remain." What we learn is how inescapably we are all prisoners of our own pasts. The extraordinary thing is that in the very course of becoming aware of the prison, we achieve a new freedom.

In a sober vein people can be called scoundrels, I think, when they refuse to face the child within them, when they refuse to acknowledge their own past. Perhaps they are most truly scoundrels when they refuse to recognize that they remain human beings throughout their lives, and are never the gods they sometimes pretend to be.

The problems in this area involve not only the rate of growth and the degree of maturation. Some are also posed by the hypocrisy to which Keniston called our attention. Put in positive terms, we are concerned here not only with maturation, but also with what contemporary existentialists often call *authenticity,* what the young mean by "doing their own thing." We are prisoners of our own pasts, to be sure, but we may be even more helplessly shackled by an oppressive present which we are powerless to change. In the degree to which the roles we act out are those which have been assigned to us, not those we have ourselves freely chosen, we are living only as involuntary selves. Such, at least, is the experience of a great many students, and, quite understandably, of many draftees.

Even when the roles are of our own choosing, there are still the problems of redefining our individualities in terms of the redefinitions in our time of the roles themselves. There is no doubt that the very conception of most of our roles has been changing radically, and at a fantastically rapid pace. What does it mean today to be a woman in our society? Or to

Concluding Remarks

be a parent? An intellectual? A good citizen? I think that Lord Robbins was very right in emphasizing the realistic basis of the uneasiness we all know so well in the young. When the present is so indeterminate, uncertainty as to the future is quite realistic; it is especially realistic when we are powerless to guide the emerging future.

This leads us directly to a second aspect of our subject, beyond the psychological one.

Our discussions have repeatedly raised the question of controlling the power which technology has put into our hands. How shall we ensure—is it possible to ensure—that technology will be our servant, not our master? We have not questioned (I think rightly) the moral status of technology itself. As Friedman insisted, for instance, there is nothing wrong with television as a technology, but there is something most decidedly wrong in the use that we are making of it. Keniston's reports about the ambivalent attitudes of the radical toward modern technology are very much to the point. I venture to add that since the beginnings of technology such ambivalence has been characteristic of every thinking man. I am reminded of the pun of Heraclitus, in the sixth century B.C., on the Greek word for the archer's bow, *bios:* "Its name is life, and its work is death."

As to the specific bearings of technology on individuality, or even more generally on the distinctively human quality of our lives, we have had little to say. Automation, for example, was barely mentioned; we only just touched on what Norbert Wiener called the "cybernetic revolution." There has been much loose talk in our society about how the computer technology is freeing man at last for the unfolding of all his potentialities, as though the brave new world is already here. Wiener himself often emphasized that the cybernetic revolution has not yet freed us. The fact is that most of the world's population, as well as a significant fraction of the American population, has not yet been freed even by the industrial revolution. For most people—even in our affluent society, to say nothing of the rest of the world—work is still a deadening routine of meaningless operations directed toward trivial ends. Certainly the work of education—which is what most of us know best, whether as teachers or as students—often has this character.

With regard to the prospects for the development and expression of individuality, we Americans are surely among the most favored of men; but how much is yet wanting! We can all respond willingly to André Gide's stipulation that we produce only what is in us. But when we are alienated from the instruments of production, alienated from control over its conditions, and alienated from decisions as to its consequences, our willingness is of no avail.

Technology confronts us with a quite fundamental dilemma, which several of the panelists have touched on. We cannot survive in the modern world *without* our technology, but it is a real question now whether we can survive *with* it. Aristotle, with characteristic simplicity and wisdom, once pointed out that before a man can live well he must be able to live. It is the question of the possibility of life itself which

Concluding Remarks

is now on man's agenda. Many times in the past, men have talked about the imminent end of the world; in our time, for the first time, this is no longer just talk. If we are not destroyed by a nuclear cataclysm, we may yet succumb to the slower but just as deadly processes by which we are poisoning our food, our water, and our air. The ecological crisis is the inescapable background to all other human problems.

Humanizing our technology is at least in part a political matter. The panel has brought out a number of political aspects of the problem of individuality.

In our discussions a good deal of attention was paid to the political control of the market. I was struck by how much less attention was paid to the control of thought. Had we been meeting a decade or so ago to discuss individuality, I think there would have been considerable talk about widespread pressures to conform, subtle techniques for engineering consent, and the pervasive influences molding thought and opinion. Our silence on these matters may be a sign that individualism is in much less danger today than it was then. The silence may be, on the other hand, a sign that we have resigned ourselves to these dangers, and feel helpless to ward them off.

We did touch on something which comes near the very core of individuality: the preservation of a zone of privacy. Justice Louis Brandeis once called privacy the most comprehensive of rights, the one most precious to civilized beings. There is coming to be considerable awareness of the dangers to privacy in the new technologies of electronic surveillance, computerized files of personal information, and the like. Although such developments obviously have an enormous bearing on the problems of individuality we have been discussing, we did not elaborate on the issues they raise. Possible conflicts between individual rights and social interests were considered here chiefly in connection with Friedman's thesis that social interests are best served merely by protection of individual rights. There would be no conflict, he was saying, if only we let things alone. For my part (though I could not begin to sketch a case as brilliantly persuasive as Friedman's), I find it hard to believe in preestablished harmonies underlying society, and uninviting to think of the individual as essentially a self-respecting customer. To be sure, one aspect of individuality *is* constituted by the free choices of a consumer. But I am convinced that other models than those formulated in terms of the market place will contribute more to our understanding of what we cherish as individuality.

We came closer to the dimension of individuality I have in mind here when Lipset talked about the tendency in the radical right to treat the enemy as a non-person. I see this tendency in some elements of the militant left as well. It seems to me absolutely crucial that however we define "the enemy," we still see him as a person. The declaration to which I would have us all commit ourselves is: "I will not be inhuman for the sake of humanity, I will not destroy the other in order to save him." This implies that I will not destroy his mind to save his thinking, deny him a choice in

Concluding Remarks

order to make sure that he does not choose wrongly. Freedom, it seems to me, is inseparable from the right to make mistakes.

Finally, there is a moral aspect to our problem which we have discussed many times, though not in explicitly ethical terms. Society is impossible without some people exercising power over others. How is power to be exercised morally? Is it intrinsically even compatible with morality?

Just after the First World War, A. E. Housman published a poem from which a whole generation of novelists took titles. The poet described himself as "a stranger and afraid, in a world I never made." I suppose that there have always been people who felt this way about their world. Young people today certainly feel that they live in a world not of their making. The remarkable thing is that they are not afraid of this world in which they are strangers. They are resolved to make the best of it even so, to make the world more nearly one in which man can feel at home. We know that they are often disillusioned. Yet the aspiration to subject power to morality can guide action without risking despair. "The moral man enters politics," Confucius said, "not because he expects his principles to prevail, but because it is in accord with his principles to enter politics."

The question is, what are these principles, or what should they be? It seems to me that in our time every dialogue concerning individuality, especially every dialogue in which the young participate, involves this question at least implicitly. "What should I do now, in my situation? I am very much inclined to do such-and-such; I feel strongly that for me it is the right thing to do, that I not only *may* do it but that I *ought* to do it. Please tell me, am I not right? Shouldn't I go ahead?" If we are candid, I think we will admit that at one time or another we all ask for such advice, or more likely, for support for decisions already taken, and for reassurance as to what will follow in consequence. The irony lies in seeking to express individuality by asking another, "Please show me how I can be myself!"

Nietzsche's Zarathustra proclaims, "This is *my* way; what is yours? As for *the* way, it does not exist." That expression of individuality is only one side of the matter; there is a social side as well. Each of us must go his own way, to be sure. It may be, however, that we can so order our lives and our resources—all the resources we have been discussing: the psychological, the technological, the political—that for some part of our journeys we can go our ways together.